If These WALLS *Could* TALK: PITTSBURGH STEELERS

Stories from the Pittsburgh Steelers Sideline, Locker Room, and Press Box

Craig Wolfley
with Jim Wexell

TRIUMPH
BOOKS

To my dear wife, Faith.
I love you forever, then some, and more.

Library of Congress Cataloging-in-Publication Data available upon request.

This book is available in quantity at special discounts for your group or organization. For further information, contact:

Triumph Books LLC
814 North Franklin Street
Chicago, Illinois 60610
(312) 337-0747
www.triumphbooks.com

Printed in U.S.A.
ISBN: 978-1-63727-763-8
Production by Patricia Frey

All photographs courtesy of the author unless otherwise noted.

Praise for Craig Wolfley and *If These Walls Could Talk: Pittsburgh Steelers*

"We only played one year together, but it turned into a lifelong friendship. Why, just read the book! Like me, you will fall in love with the man. He worked hard, he was driven, he succeeded, but he was still just the Wolfman—down-to-earth, a lineman at heart with his own made-up vocabulary. More importantly, he captured the essence of what a Steeler was and should be."

—Rocky Bleier, former Steelers teammate

"The Wolfman took uniqueness to a new level. A funny man who didn't try to be funny, his gift of being able to relate to Steelers fans was obvious when he played and during the all-too-brief time we were privileged to share with him as a broadcaster. We miss No. 73."

—Bill Hillgrove, Voice of the Steelers, 1994–2024

"I'm a lucky guy. My life's journey crossed paths with one of the great teammates in life and with the Pittsburgh Steelers: Craig Wolfley. He was always colorful in the huddle, on the field, in the locker room, and when broadcasting. I know of no one more genuine, kind, funny, and willing to fight for others like Wolf; he always had my back, and I knew it. He lived a selfless life, and we are lucky he left some of his great memories for all of us to treasure."

—Merril Hoge, former Steelers teammate and media colleague

"Howl like a wolf! It was my honor to know and learn from the Wolfman. He was a man of faith and family, someone I never saw without a smile. His love of Christ, football, and the Steelers became his life's work, but his real victories are the people he influenced along the way. *If These Walls Could Talk* inspires both howls of laughter and feelings of mourning for the great man whose impact left us all better than he found us."

—Brett Keisel, former Steeler and friend

"If you want to get to know Wolf, read this book. His passion for football and love for the Steelers come through on every page."

—Bob Labriola, Steelers team historian

"Craig Wolfley was Pittsburgh's big brother, uncle, friend, or whatever you needed him to be on that day. He interjected into our lives like a 'ballistic enema' for good! Heaven gained a tremendous man and Pittsburgh lost a true champion. Thankfully he left us these stories."

—Max Starks, former Steeler and talk show partner

CONTENTS

FOREWORD

BY RON WOLFLEY

If you have ever met Craig, you know Craig. He was the most straightforward, what-you-see-is-what-you-get human being I have ever known.

And there was *so much* to see.

Craig was a walking, talking World's Fair freak show. At 6'2", 320 pounds, my older brother was a larger-than-life paradox, walking down the midway of life. He played 12 years in the National Football League, competed in the World's Strongest Man contest, owned and operated a full-contact martial arts center for 20 years, was a black belt in freestyle jujitsu, trained people in the sport of ultimate fighting and how to choke people out on the mat.... Yet all he did was walk through his day loving people, hugging people, and making them feel special.

"Step right up, ladies and gentlemen! See the man destroy common expectations! Watch a man bear-hug an unsuspecting person! See the man look into people's eyes, smile, and speak encouraging words! See the man they call *the Big Dog*!"

It is not the physical, carny-like presence of my older brother Craig that I will miss the most. It's his simple-man wisdom, rooted in God's Word, I will miss. Like the time when I was nervous about going to the first-ever national NFL Combine in Tempe, Arizona, in 1985. I was speaking with Craig on the phone, and he could tell I was distracted.

"Ronnie, are you okay?" Craig said.

"Yeah, I just hope I run a good 40 time at the combine. I haven't been able to train the way I've wanted to and I—"

"Ronnie, if God doesn't want you to play in the NFL, you are going to run the fastest 40 time you have ever run, and you're not going to play a down. And if God does want you to play in the NFL, you are going to run the slowest 40 time you've ever run and play 15 years in the league."

I can still hear his gravelly voice thumping through my ears. It is like a warm blanket to me on a cold winter night. His advice was said in

My brother Ronnie and I meet up on the field after a game between the Steelers and Cardinals.

love, spot-on, filled with strength, and relaxed me; I ran the fastest 40 I'd ever run.

This was just one small example of the love Craig showed to me and everybody in the family. He showed his love for us by listening to our concerns, considering them carefully, using his wisdom and life experiences to advise us, and then telling us what we needed to hear—and he did it in love. He cared for others before he cared for himself, a servant leader who took the time to pour that love into friends and family.

Love is strength, and strength is love, and Craig loved God and loved people.

To *know* Craig is to know how hard he tried to model his King, Jesus Christ. Although he failed many times, as we all do, it was the physical and spiritual juxtaposition of Craig that makes me think of my King, Jesus Christ. Nobody was stronger than Jesus of Nazareth, and yet He gave His life for us in the name of love so that we might have life. Isn't that right, Craig?

—In loving memory, Ronnie

INTRODUCTION

BY JIM WEXELL

I think about the late Craig Wolfley more often than I expected. I'm writing this introduction to Craig's book two days after the completion of the 2025 NFL Draft, so I'll just use that weekend as an example:

I think about when I walked past radio row inside the Steelers' South Side facility. Craig, no matter whether he was on air or off, would always exclaim, "Hey, Wex!" When my podcast partner called a fourth-rounder an "apex predator," I knew he was honoring Craig. When someone mangled the name of fifth-round pick Yahya Black, I knew Craig would've just called him "Mr. Black." And when someone at dinner said, "I'll have the rest of that steak if you're not going to eat it," I could hear Craig laugh as he was already reaching for it.

Really, all joking aside, I think of Craig in my more serious moments too, like when I need good advice, some of his nonjudgmental wisdom.

"Keep Jesus close, brother" was the last thing he said to me. He said it from his hospital bed when we both thought—or at least he had convinced *me* to think—that his situation was only temporary. But his life abruptly ended on the same day this manuscript was due at Triumph Books headquarters.

Of course, the publishing house had given us a bit of an extension when Craig fell ill 20 days earlier. They were shocked, as we all were, to hear the sad news that on March 10, 2025, Craig Alan Wolfley left us.

Craig did supply us with these 70,000 cherished words before he parted. Being a part of that process, I saw on full display what made him such a great teammate. He didn't wait until the deadline to get his work done. In fact, the only tardy work was mine, and to tell you the truth, that wasn't much.

About 20 years ago, when Craig moved on from his post-playing days as gym owner to become the Steelers' sideline reporter, he wanted to begin writing his memoirs of a Buffalo lad turned Syracuse man turned Steeler for life.

Craig, a new acquaintance of mine, sent me sample chapters and asked whether they had book potential. I told him yes, and that I was so impressed with his skills I would like to hire him to write for my publication, *SteelCityInsider*.

He wrote a weekly column for the next 20 years. And when Triumph called with an idea for *If These Walls Could Talk*, a book they wanted written by a Steelers lifer, someone who could span the Chuck Noll–Bill Cowher–Mike Tomlin eras, I had only one candidate for them: Wolf.

Because Craig was an outstanding offensive guard through the 1980s, and has been watching not only games but practices throughout the 1990s and 2000s, he was perfect. Besides, he could write.

Triumph was thrilled because Wolf was perfect for their vision. What was perfect for me was that Triumph would pay me just as much as Craig, since, in theory, I would ghostwrite for the former athlete. But as the former athlete called the 2024 Steelers games from the press box on Thursdays, Sundays, and Mondays, he wrote book chapters from his basement on Tuesdays. The chapters poured in. I pretty much ignored those emails, saving them for when the work was to begin in January upon the completion of the Steelers season I was also covering.

However, waiting to work wasn't in Wolf's DNA. After the Steelers were eliminated from playoff contention, I wrote to tell Craig it was time to work. He wrote back and asked if I had received all the chapters he had sent. I looked, and, holy —, this freakin' book was done!

Triumph scheduled a conference call a week later in order to gauge our progress. I told them that the book was just about finished but that I was stealing their money, that Craig should be getting all of it since there was no "ghostwriting for the athlete" involved here.

"Oh, no, Wex," Craig interjected. "Let's stick with the original deal. Please."

That's just one example of Craig's generosity and character. In fact, there are at least 36 more examples awaiting you in the 36 chapters that unfold in this book. There are lessons for kids about playing a game, and there are lessons for adults about living life. There are stories that will make you laugh and stories that will no doubt elicit tears as we think about the man we have lost.

Upon Craig's death, this book became a special project of mine, as well as of Craig's widow, Faith. She wanted me to continue the project, and was thrilled when I asked if she and her family could help. I am so proud to have their bylines inside these pages, with son C. J.'s "Wolf Lists" also included.

Thankfully, Craig has left us with these life lessons, these great stories. I can only hope that, as editor, I didn't get in the way.

—Jim Wexell

CHAPTER 1

END OF THE INNOCENCE

Walking into the Steelers' locker room as a rookie fifth-round draft pick back in 1980 was, obviously, a big moment for me. Well, actually, it really wasn't that big of a deal, because the locker room itself wasn't that big of a deal. The facilities at St. Vincent College had been built for college athletes. And, just like the penal colony–like dorm rooms in which we'd stay, they were smallish, stark, and rather unremarkable—not at all what I had envisioned after being drafted by the four-time world champions.

I reported for the first week of fully padded double sessions in mid-July 1980. After checking into training camp and spending the first week with all the other rookies and selected early-report veterans, I finally got to meet the rest of the veterans as they reported. What had once been ample space was suddenly an elbow-to-elbow bottleneck. As expected, my locker was in the low-rent rookie section, where crowding was at a max; the vets had the slightly larger, more spacious area in which they could manspread a little.

There was plenty of excitement in watching these legends and future Hall of Famers report for duty and prepare for practice. Getting to meet the guys I had grown up watching was almost overwhelming. I mean, what do you say when you see guys like "Mean" Joe Greene, Jack Lambert, Terry Bradshaw, Mike Webster, Franco Harris, and Jon Kolb up close and personal as they go about the process of "boarding up" for practice?

Rookies back then were often looked upon as those who should be seen and not heard. The vets would tolerate you enough to welcome you—as in, "Hey, rook"—but engaging rookies in anything more than passing conversation wasn't exactly the norm.

Walking into the locker room for the first time with the vets was like walking into your first job interview—but with multiple people checking you out rather than a select one or two. Over the years I would come to recognize the signs of fear, nervousness, and shyness oozing from the

In my rookie season with the Steelers. Courtesy of the Pittsburgh Steelers

young bucks who wanted nothing more than to be accepted by the vets. And I'm sure I projected the same in my rookie camp as well. Coming somewhat trepidatiously into the locker room, I felt as if suddenly all eyes had turned and latched on to me, as if I were being introduced as a non-friendly in need of a Code Red–style beatdown. I could have heard a pin drop as the conversation stopped and I was eyeballed. I tried to convince myself that all of the conversations didn't suddenly stop when I walked in, or that I suddenly seemed to be someone at whom everyone was staring in that moment. But it was uncomfortable, and, really, the silence was more than a mere perception.

I tried to ignore the rapidly rising red-faced blush and awkward feeling that had washed over me and go about my business of boarding up. As I turned to my locker, I heard a booming voice from behind me. It was Steelers defensive legend L. C. Greenwood. He loudly cleared his throat and said, "Young buck, that shirt ain't gonna fly around here for very long."

That's when I realized my blunder, what all the uncomfortable stares and double takes had been about. I had thrown on a T-shirt that fellow Buffalonian and Philadelphia Eagles quarterback Ron Jaworski had given me before I was drafted by the Steelers. It was an Eagles T-shirt. With a big Eagles emblem on the front. I hadn't even bothered to check what I was wearing; it was just the next shirt up in my suitcase.

The true testing period was about to come. In fact, it was the very next morning, with the first of 12 consecutive padded practices over the first six days. And while I eventually learned in the throes of a brutal Chuck Noll–run training camp that wardrobe and personal hygiene tend to take a back seat to eating, sleeping, being on time, and walking without a limp, I had obviously much more to learn. Like simple logic.

I pretended I hadn't heard L. C. and kept on going about my business. Apparently, that's when L.C.'s game plan began to come together. Nearly three hours later, after coming off the practice field, drained of all ability to coherently think, I slumped down on the stool in front of my locker. Slowly I began the cumbersome process of "de-boarding," or stripping off my practice jersey, shoulder pads, and such.

Weary as only a Chuck Noll double-session practice can make you, I took my time heading into the shower and then getting dressed before heading to the dining hall for supper. Most of the locker room had already cleared out, as the vets hurried off to their favorite watering holes to "replenish fluids," as Noll always urged the players to do. Though I don't think Chuck was talking about replenishing fluids with foamy adult beverages.

As I reached for my T-shirt, I suddenly noticed it wasn't there. I rummaged around, shoving my equipment to one side of the narrow locker to which I had been assigned. Hmmm...nothing. Well...where in the world was—And then it dawned on me. L. C. was spot-on with his prediction of the sustainability of that T-shirt in the very heart of Steelers Country. At that moment I realized that my T-shirt had indeed flown the coop. The gift from my hometown area's local legend was gone, *oof!*, never to be seen again.

No, I didn't ask for it back. Are you kidding? Life was tough enough for me as it was, locking horns with all these great players on a daily basis. As for L. C., the smile and booming laugh that greeted me when I saw him next was enough for me to know he had been the culprit. While they may sing "Fly, Eagles, Fly" in Philly, in locker rooms throughout Steelers Country, it was always "Bye, Eagles, Bye."

CHAPTER 2

CHUCK NOLL AND THE ART OF THE PUNCH

Way back before the turn of the century, during my senior year at Syracuse University, I came face-to-face with some very sobering statistics. One of them went like this: The chance of making it in the NFL at that time was roughly 1 in 140,000. Even for a guy like me, who flunked math twice, those odds seemed to be fairly insurmountable—to say the least. To top it off, check this out: The average career length of an NFL player was approximately 3.2 years. So, realistically, the odds were that I was never going to get there, and, if I did, the ride would be a short one.

I didn't have to be a math whiz to realize I had to make the most of every opportunity. Like the one that came in the pre-spring days of 1980 at Manley Field House on campus, when the coach of the four-time Super Bowl–champion Pittsburgh Steelers came to work me out. Me. By myself. With no other teammates.

To say I was overwhelmed would be putting it lightly. Me and the Emperor, as legendary broadcaster Myron Cope had dubbed Chuck Noll, would be working out mano a mano. But it was time to show off what I had, to find a way to make it memorable. It would be a personal workout, but I had no idea just how personal it would get.

We went through a couple of run-blocking drills. After the run-blocking techniques were explained and then performed to some degree of satisfaction, we moved on to pass protection. Coach Noll began lining up across from me, physically pass-rushing me. All the while, he was instructing me on the art of the punch, a recent development that had come along with an NFL rule change. No longer would offensive linemen be "heavy bags on two feet," subjected to head slaps from the pass rusher. No longer would they have to hold their hands against their chests in pass protection. Using the hands to "punch" the pass rusher, to keep him from grabbing you, was a technique Coach Noll was attempting to teach me. As a matter of fact, the power punch had been pioneered a couple years earlier by then–Steelers offensive line coach Dan "Bad Rad" Radakovich and developed by Steelers legends Jon Kolb and Larry Brown. And it was ultimately perfected by my brother from another mother Tunch Ilkin.

But I knew none of this at the time. I was dressed simply in shorts and a T-shirt, Coach Noll in a Steelers golf shirt and pants, that day we met. No helmets, pads, none of that. Coach Noll began by explaining the technique, and then demonstrated it. Then came the walk-through, and then the pace quickened. After several awkward one-on-one physical matchups with Coach Noll, I sensed a mounting frustration on his part. I could hear the tinges of it in his voice as he upped the intensity of each rush. There I was, working on punching techniques with a future

It didn't take me long to perfect the art of the punch. Here I am standing up to an Baltimore Colt.
Courtesy of the Pittsburgh Steelers

Hall of Famer, the head coach of the Pittsburgh Steelers, who had just won a fourth Super Bowl, and I wasn't getting it.

Now, you must understand Coach Noll. He was first and foremost a teacher before he was a football coach. He prized teaching the basic elements of football and thoroughly communicating them in clear and precise terms that anyone could understand. At least they were clear in his mind. And if it seemed that the teaching wasn't getting through to whomever, there would be a noticeable rise in the anxiety level of that whomever as Chuck bore down. Believe me, when Coach Noll fixated on you in a teaching situation, he inspired genuine fear and anxiety. If you think I'm exaggerating, ask Joe Greene, who once said Chuck could give you a look that would make you pee down your leg.

And that player who was feeling a rise in his anxiety level (and perhaps some bladder control issues too) was me in that moment. The agitation Coach was feeling at this particular time was directed solely at me because he knew I was holding back. I feared that this job interview was about to go south. After another rather pedestrian, senior-citizen-speed rush by Chuck, and a half-hearted pass-pro punch by me, Chuck side-eyed me again. I was now feeling the Noll-induced anxiety growing feverishly in my gut. Because, hey, how hard was I supposed to punch a living legend nearly twice my age? To say I was conflicted would be a huge understatement.

After a few more semi-scowls crossed the face of Coach Noll, I knew I was on borrowed time. Finally, Chuck lined up in a three-point stance across from me and fairly growled, "Now let me feel you *punch* me!" I knew it was now or never. In an escalating state of panic, I put my hand on the turf, and Chuck rushed and threw an uppercut and I punched him. *Boom!* I mean, I let him have it. It was a well-timed howitzer of a punch with all of my then-455-pound-bench-press strength behind it. Unfortunately for both of us, I was a little errant. My right hand glanced off Chuck's shoulder and popped him in the mouth. His head snapped back like a Pez dispenser. I had hit him right in the grill, and he abruptly came to a screaming halt in the process of pass rushing. I was already cringing when I noticed I had drawn blood. Surely this interview process was about to be over, and Chuck Noll, the Pittsburgh Steelers, and I were about to go our separate ways.

Slowly, Chuck turned toward me. I saw that flare of the squinted eyebrows and the famous bulldog look that I would come to know over the years whenever I screwed up. With my heart beating a zillion times a minute, Chuck touched his suddenly swollen lip, looked at the trickle of blood on his fingertips, and a smile broke out on his face. He looked right at me, nodded his head, and said emphatically, "Now *that's* a punch." When I got back to my apartment after the workout, I called my parents and glumly told them, "We can take the Steelers off the draft board. No way do they draft me."

Several weeks later the NFL Draft rolled around. I spent most of the first day sitting by a phone that only rang when my grandma called to see if I had been drafted. At five o'clock in the afternoon, the draft officially shut down for the day. I wasn't totally unprepared for a first-day snub; in fact, I had been told by my college coach, Frank Maloney, that the pro scouts thought I would be a second-day or free agent after 12 completed rounds. But I'd always been a glass-half-full guy and was a little dejected when I left the house. About 30 minutes later, the phone rang at my house and my younger sister Joy (around 12 years old at the time) picked it up. She listened momentarily and then began chatting up the person on the other end of the line. After several minutes, my mother asked her who she was talking to. Joy frowned, gave her a thumbs-down gesture, covered the mouthpiece with her hand, and said simply, "Some guy from Pittsburgh named Chuck."

And that's how I came to be drafted by the Pittsburgh Steelers in the fifth round back in 1980. Of course, I would be remiss if I didn't mention the fact that my aforementioned brother Tunch was drafted in the very same draft, but in the *sixth* round. Not to be competitive. As Tunch would say with a laugh, at least he graduated and wasn't just an attendee. We both conquered some pretty stiff odds, didn't we? One out of 140,000, in fact. And it's gotta be triple that when you punch your future coach in the mouth.

CHAPTER 3

WHEN THE MAGIC HAPPENED

I turned the corner of the stadium alcove, and the sight was unforgettable. In fact, I was stunned, even at my young age. Looking into the lights that shone down on the field from high above, I was illuminated by a world more raw, raucous, and magical than I ever could have imagined. Football unfolded before me in the form of a ballistic cacophony that thrilled me, held me in awe, and instantly crystallized what I wanted to do with my life: play professional football. Full stop.

I was around 12 years old and hadn't done anything but ride dirt bikes, play neighborhood ball with friends, and eat chicken wings in my hometown of Orchard Park, a suburb of Buffalo, New York. One of five siblings, three boys and two girls, I was second-born to my parents, Ron and Esther Wolfley, on May 19, 1958. I had a great childhood. We weren't wealthy, but none of us ever felt deprived.

My younger brothers grew to share the same love of football that I did, and we'd watch some football on TV with my dad. My first memory of a personal encounter with a pro player back then was at a local hardware store. Bills wide receiver Haven Moses was there signing autographs. My mother drove me there, dropped me off, and I was so awestruck it took a good hour or so to finally approach Haven for an autograph. I don't know why I was so shy at the time, but it certainly was a memory that stuck with me. Haven Moses was 10 feet tall in my eyes.

My love of football was well-known among my family members. For instance, though I wasn't quite sure what a first down was, my mom tells the story of seven-year-old me, who had told her secretly that I was "gonna play pro football someday." Out of the mouths of babes, indeed. God sure put that desire in my heart early.

Even though I loved the game, I had never played any organized ball at any level before I saw my first pro game. But on this night, at the stadium alcove, I was just a young guy from Orchard Park on a church youth group outing to watch the Bills. Along with a bunch of my friends,

A throwback to my high school days with the Orchard Park Quakers.

I found myself standing in the alcove entryway of the upper stands of War Memorial Stadium in northeast Buffalo. Brock Yates of *Sports Illustrated* jokingly wrote in 1969 that the stadium looked "as if whatever war it was a memorial to had been fought within its confines." The stadium had opened in 1937 and been known by various names over the years. Best known as the Rockpile, it was highlighted in, and made famous by, the Robert Redford baseball movie *The Natural.*

Criticism of the stadium was totally warranted. The locker rooms, more like oversized closets, were way too small to house 40-plus players and showers. And those showers only functioned on a part-time basis. Girders used in the construction made some of the sight lines difficult in certain parts of the field. And parts of the field froze over, while other parts didn't due to, I suppose, poor planning. (I mean, how could that be a problem in balmy Buffalo, New York?) Even getting on and off the field could be a problem. The Dodge Street Tunnel had fans seated extremely close to the players, and when the players exited and entered the stadium, beer cans frequently rained down on them. Then there was the neighborhood surrounding the stadium. It was a rough area of town. Night games were a little dicey.

The Bills had captured the AFL championship in 1964 with a win over San Diego at War Memorial Stadium. The 1966 AFL title game, which was also played at the Rockpile, saw the Bills lose to the Chiefs, who went on to play in the inaugural Super Bowl. After joining the NFL in 1970, the Bills found themselves needing a better venue. The stadium sat only 46,000 fans, and NFL brass required a minimum of 50,000. That's why the Bills moved to Orchard Park, and their new stadium, in 1973.

But to me—at my first professional game in the first professional stadium I had ever visited—it was fantasyland. It might as well have been Disney World. I was mesmerized. The fact it was a night game made it all the more magical. The names were O. J. Simpson, Haven

Moses, Mike Stratton, Al Cowlings, Ron McDole, and big, thumping, 254-pound fullback Wayne Patrick. Veteran quarterback Jack Kemp led the offense. Watching live, there in the confines of that old warhorse of a stadium rather than just seeing it on TV, was an eye-opening experience. The guys who were on a grocery store poster on the back of my bedroom door came alive on the field. I knew all of them and could easily recite their pertinent stats.

This was a glorious time of pure fandom, a time to collect playing cards and posters, along with their official league portraits. I loved their action shots, in which a player might be diving while in full pads but with no helmet. Another guy would be taking a knee, and still others were doing a Heisman pose or catching imaginary passes. Of course, they were staged action shots, but I loved them all.

Finances and Sunday afternoon games had previously discouraged any attendance on my part, but my desire to attend a game never waned. So when I finally got the chance to be there in person, it instantly became a moment in time that's never left me. If I close my eyes and lean back in my chair, I can re-create that scintillating moment in my mind's eye like it was yesterday. That night, the Bills were playing the Boston Patriots, before they were the New England Patriots and way before anyone had heard of Robert Kraft, Bill Belichick, or Tom Brady. (Yes, that far back.)

I turned that corner after walking up the outer ramp to the inner world of the stands and the screaming fans, and I became transfixed. The lights, the loudspeakers, the game roaring before me in the echoes of the crowd are stamped in my mind. It was the greatest thing I had ever seen. I was watching virtually the equivalent of a human demolition derby, with massive men wearing colorful uniforms crashing their bodies into one another as an air of excitement swept through the crowd.

Pro football. That first encounter with it set the course for the rest of my life. At that moment, I knew, just knew, that somehow this was where I was going. Not into the stands...not to just cheer on my hometown team...not to collect trading cards, pictures, and posters. No, I needed to get on that field, to be a part of that chaotic violence. And let me tell you, what a ride it's been.

CHAPTER 4
THANKSGIVING DAY MASSACRE

There are many ways to tell if a football game is going badly without looking at the scoreboard. Coughing up turnovers like phlegm is always a sign. Giving up sacks in banana bunches. Not seeing the other side of the field until the quarter ends. And just as there are indicators, there are forewarnings of those indicators. The sudden onset of illness. Poor practices throughout the week. A general feeling of malaise as game time approaches. Things like that can leave an ominous feeling in the gullet as game day approaches.

But I gotta say, dumping jet fuel over the Great Lakes on the way to a game had never been one I'd considered—until Mike Webster pointed it out as we flew toward Detroit for a Thanksgiving Day game in 1983. "I don't know about you," said Iron Mike, looking out the window while tightly gripping the back of the seat ahead of him, "but I sure don't like the looks of that. That's a bad sign, boys."

Man, did he call that one right. While flying over the Great Lakes toward Detroit, we watched the plane send extra fuel, or whatever it was, pouring out over the wings. It gave me those pregame heebie-jeebies, a sense that things were not all copacetic in the football universe.

The NFL's Thanksgiving Day schedule of games has consisted of a Detroit Lions home game since 1934 (excepting a six-year stretch during World War II). The league added a Dallas Cowboys home game in 1966. As a player, it was a cool experience the first time around, and that's how I felt about this one—at first. Aside from the fact I would be away from family and friends, playing before the entire country on the big stage was big for this young guy from Orchard Park. Over my career, I played on Thanksgiving, Christmas, Christmas Eve, New Year's Eve, and of course New Year's Day, and it's all pretty much the same. While you're hundreds of miles from home busting your hump in a stadium with thousands of diehard fans, everybody else is slipping into a food coma.

The fuel dump was unnerving, but the unsettling feelings had already pervaded my mind earlier in the week. My teammate and roommate on

(Left to right) Webby, me, and Tunch deplane after a getaway to Canada.

the road, Tunch Ilkin, was sick with the flu; he had even spent a night in the hospital. This was back when it was up to the player to decide whether he could play or not. And you know what that meant: Unless something was sticking out at a dysfunctional angle or you were so sick you couldn't see straight, you were going to suit up and get the job done.

I was drafted onto a Steelers team that was loaded with veterans. The Joe Greenes, Mike Websters, Jon Kolbs, Larry Browns, and Jack Lamberts were all renowned tough guys who set a certain standard, and obviously all of us young guys wanted to live up to that standard.

Playing on Thanksgiving means it's already a short week, so the chances of Tunch getting a solid recovery by game time were slim to none. Frankly, job one was to get Tunch into another room, all by himself and quarantined, because the last thing I wanted was to sleep in the same room with him and wind up sick myself. He's my brother, and I am my brother's keeper, for sure, but quarantining was the right call on this trip.

So after the weird flight to Detroit and a not-so-great night of sleep, I went through the pregame machinations in preparation for a game that would get out of control straight from the get-go. We kicked off at half past noon, Central time. And for all intents and purposes, the game was over five minutes later.

There are times when, as a veteran player, you know how to read the room and see that things not only aren't going your way but disastrously so. And the harder you try to turn things around, the worse things get. This was one of those days. The samurai sixth sense veterans develop over years of playing was sensing something wicked this way comes. And as the saying goes, buckle up, baby, because it's about to drop.

And, boy, did it ever. We were swept away by a Lions team that had won five of its last seven games—they picked off five Steelers passes, returned a punt for a touchdown (by a player who had been drafted and cut by the Steelers), and outhit us in every way imaginable.

The Lions scored on their first four possessions of the game. *Boom, boom, boom, and boom.* The great Billy Sims got it started with the first TD, as he went on to gain more than 100 yards in the game. He was in a zone—particularly one play, in which he took the handoff, ran off tackle, and between zigs and zags leaped into the air, planted his foot on the head of the great Jack Lambert, and actually cut off his helmet.

That's right. No misprint. You talk about a back "sticking his foot in the ground"—well, this was a new one. I saw the skid mark on Lambert's lid with my own eyes at halftime. Unbelievable. I mean, how do you stop a guy who can cut off helmets? In trying to make those early-game tackles, I momentarily felt like I was back on the punt cover team.

After that opening drive, the crowd, as if they could sense what was to come, reached one of the loudest, absolutely most boisterous and overwhelming noise levels I've ever encountered.

Our quarterback of record on this horrendous day was Cliff Stoudt. Poor guy. With Terry Bradshaw still recovering from an elbow issue (despite the best efforts of the training staff, doctors, and the infamous Myron Cope's mynah bird intervention), Cliff started the game and threw four interceptions, two of which occurred on the opening two series. But this wasn't about Cliff. Or Mark Malone. Or even Bradshaw. This was all about an entire team not playing well.

The roar of the crowd at the Pontiac Silverdome swelled and grew as the Lions mounted a 17–0 first-quarter lead. Our offense staggered around like we already had our bellies full of turkey and the tryptophan was kicking in. Our offense was on the bench so often they should have brought in couches. The defense was just as bad; they couldn't get off the field.

Halftime brought temporary relief. After all, it's hard to give up points from the locker room. I don't remember Chuck's speech, but just imagine that locker room. We were laying a giant egg on national TV, and there was Noll with a serious scowl on his face. Meanwhile, Lambert was honked off and smoking, both literally and figuratively. Bryan Hinkle was walking by with raised eyebrows like a man who couldn't believe he had to go back out for the second half. Tunch was in the corner shivering. (He probably should've been in a hospital but had "cowboyed up" and played.) Mike Webster was just shaking his head and searching for his tin of Skoal. Guys were limping around with their heads down because nobody wanted to make eye contact with anyone else. A number of players had gone down in the first half with injuries. The atmosphere was as stagnant and putrid as our first-half performance.

Lingering in that stuffy locker room was a generally unsaid feeling that with the score already 24–3, the game was all but over. It wasn't just the numbers that told the story of how inept we were, but how they'd been rolled up. As an offense, we had a harder time crossing midfield than did the Israelites crossing the Jordan River into the Promised Land. Only twice in the first half did we manage to stagger past the 50-yard line, once due to a fumble recovery on that side by our defense. Overall, it was a pretty grim-faced team looking at a lot of grim-faced coaches.

It was at this moment of deep introspection and reflection that defensive end Keith "Skippy" Willis took it upon himself to take action. Keith was a defensive leader and a great player in the making, but it was a halftime moment that he might've wished he had sat out.

"Too many guys are hurting and taking the easy way out!" exclaimed Skippy. "Sure, things are bad, but we can come back!" His voice grew louder, like an old Baptist minister addressing his mesmerized Sunday morning flock. In a voice that carried passion and emotion, he said, "I'm going back out there, and if anyone joins me, they better be ready to go the distance!" He punctuated that remark with a fist pump.

Our offense was apparently unimpressed, because we took the second-half kickoff and went three and out. The defense charged the field, with Keith leading the way. A lot of pep and urgency bubbled from the huddle, but disaster followed. On the second play, Keith pulled a hamstring. As he limped off the field, nose tackle Gary Dunn walked past and said, "Good speech, Skip." Oh, it was an impassioned speech, all right…with a Woody Allen finish.

Of course, there was nothing funny about the beatdown. Despite our best efforts, the second half turned out much as the first. We were awful. We couldn't run the ball and our defense couldn't stop Detroit from rolling the chains. As we came off the field after yet another three and out, with the score 31–3, I happened to be walking next to offensive tackle Larry Brown. Bubba looked at me and said, "You know what the worst part about this game is? This is only the third quarter."

Later on, quarterback Mark Malone entered the game for Stoudt. Frankly, every one of us should have been replaced. During a TV timeout, Mark tried to rally the troops in the huddle. "Come on, guys, we can do it!" Mark exclaimed with all the sincerity of a used-car salesman who knows better but has the boss standing right next to him.

Webbie, ever the pro's pro, was standing next to me in the huddle. He bent over and leaned toward me. A movie buff and a huge Bill Murray fan, Mike cracked a sideways smile. Imitating Murray's voice perfectly, he said to me, "There's no way in hell we can do it." It was a line from *Stripes*. We broke up laughing, only to quickly shut our yappers after we threw a quick glance over at Coach Noll. Wouldn't want to be caught on the job having a laugh under these conditions, especially since it was now 38–3.

All misery must come to an end, and this game was no different. After Lions backup quarterback Gary Danielson kicked what was now a black-and-gold corpse with a five-yard touchdown pass, the final score was set at 45–3. The only act of mercy shown us on this day came with 54 seconds left. Referee Gene Barth announced that the official game clock needed to be run down to 28 seconds.

Why not to zero?

"As I was walking back in here," Noll said amid an otherwise silent locker room, "I mulled over the turning point of this game. I decided it was the opening kickoff."

At such times, you just want to be left alone, hit the shower, and beat a hasty retreat to the buses. It's your only solace. With families waiting at home and meals still warm—having played an early game a relatively short distance away—I still had hope of salvaging this holiday. But on this day, the misery continued. After sitting on the buses for a while outside the airport gates, and looking for someone to take us to our plane, it was determined that our plane wasn't there. Huh? After much back-and-forth, it turned out we were at the wrong airport.

OK, maybe it was a little punishment from the football gods for giving such a lousy game to the nation. We deserved it. So, everyone climbed back on the buses and we headed out once more. We got to the right airport and went inside. After a long delay, during which everyone spent a good deal of time and effort imitating Willis's halftime speech (while making sure to keep out of hearing and sight range of the coaching staff), we were informed that our plane wouldn't start. It wouldn't even kick over. "Kind of like our offense today," someone grumped.

We killed time by "replenishing our fluids" with some adult sodas, so to speak. We were sitting around a table, about 10 of us, stacking the empty "soda" cans into a pyramid of sorts, as we rehashed the game. Nobody had more than one or two, but with all the participants, the stack of empties formed quite the pyramid.

One by one, we drifted away. Dunn, the first official nose tackle of the new 3-4 defense, was also a noted partier. That day, he was the last to leave. Noll rounded the corner and saw the stacked cans with only Gary sitting there. Chuck gave a gruff "Dunnie, I mighta known" growl under his breath and left. Gary didn't even have an opportunity to tell Chuck they weren't all his empties.

An hour or so later, we were told that the plane couldn't be fixed. We needed a mechanic, but there was another problem: They had to fly to Cleveland to get this mechanic. Yep. Mike Webster then unearthed a bigger problem than flying to Cleveland, then back to Detroit, to fix a plane bound for Pittsburgh. "Does anybody have a problem with a Cleveland mechanic working on our plane?" Webby asked no one in particular.

I called home yet again to inform waiting family members that our estimated time of arrival was somewhere closer to 11 or midnight. What else could go wrong? Hey, don't ask. We weren't even in the air yet.

Things finally got moving, and though we were tired and beat up and beat down, we finally got to home sweet home, Pittsburgh. It was late when I crossed the threshold, seeking the solace a beat-up player can only find from family. In keeping with the rest of the day, those plans were nixed. The house was quiet, the family long knocked out after a day of food, family, and fun.

I fell into my favorite double-wide La-Z-Boy chair, a pulsating throb in my left thigh causing some discomfort. The aches and pains of the day began to settle in for the night. My mind refused to slow down. It looped the day's nightmare over and over like a bad commercial jingle you can't get out of your head once you've heard it.

A little channel surfing brought Johnny Carson into the deserted living room. Yes, a little humor to end the day certainly wouldn't hurt—or so I thought. Carson came out to do his monologue with great aplomb as he took center stage. He turned and faced the crowd, and I leaned slightly forward in anticipation. "What a lousy day I had," quipped Carson. "I had the Steelers and 41 points."

Excuse me for not laughing. Time for bed, anyhow.

CHAPTER 5
MY FIRST PLAY

It's safe to say that for anyone, the first time is more meaningful than the rest, no matter what it is. For athletes, firsts are always thrilling: the first home run, the first touchdown catch, the first start in high school, college, the pros.

For an offensive lineman, the job description for a hog doesn't lean toward significant scoring plays or flashy open-field running. And your first holding call is *not* exactly a cherished memory, heaven forbid. But one cherished memory I keep is my very first play from scrimmage for the Pittsburgh Steelers. It's something I'll always remember.

I can remember the play like it was yesterday. It was my very first taste of professional football as a member of the Steelers. We were playing the New York Giants in the first preseason game of my rookie season, on Saturday, August 9, 1980, at 8:05 PM. It was in the old Giants Stadium in the swamplands of New Jersey.

The first thing I remember was getting to New York from training camp in Latrobe, Pennsylvania, which meant first driving to the Greater Pittsburgh Airport and then flying out. After roughly three weeks in Latrobe, a change of scenery was more than welcome.

But it also meant that preseason football was now officially underway, and in doing so it signaled three important shifts in life as I knew it. These same three shifts were to come each and every year in my decade with the team. First, it meant that two-a-days were over. Sweet Marie, only a survivor can appreciate the significance of putting the double sessions in the can. Young guys today who have never had the opportunity, or agony, of languishing through two-a-days often ask me how we survived. My answer is always the same: "You didn't have a choice. It's not like any of us volunteered for doubles."

Second, preseason games meant sleeping in a hotel the night before a game. Room service! Decent mattress! Not horsehair-stuffed mattresses, mind you, but built-for-a-bigger-guy mattresses rather than the flattened tortilla pallets built for skinny college dudes at St. Vincent

College. And where you could find nice mattresses and room service, you could also find the most important element of all: air-conditioning! I kid you not, nothing got me more hopped up than sleeping in an air-conditioned room.

The third consideration was the most sobering: the clock was now ticking. Cutdown dates loomed ahead. People would start disappearing. And I desperately did not want to go home.

The drive to the Pittsburgh airport from Latrobe turned out to be long, especially without GPS or cell phones. I eventually got there after a roughly two-and-a-half-hour commute to the airport, when it should've only been an hour and a half. Being a lifelong suburbanite, and inheriting my mother's sense of direction, navigating Pittsburgh was at first as foreign to me as Chinese geometry. You couldn't get there from here—or so it seemed.

After arriving in New York, I didn't look for the Statue of Liberty, nor did I hop in a cab to sightsee the Big Apple like some of the others. Nope. I went to my room, dropped the AC as low as it would go, and enjoyed a good rest. Few things create more enjoyment for fat guys than solid air-conditioning—especially when all they've had for the last several weeks is a fan blowing exhaust-pipe-quality warm air at them from six inches away while they make sweat angels on a horsehair bed. Simple pleasures go a long way in the preseason. And then there was room service. Yes, a nice steak and all the accoutrements topped off by a cherry New York–style cheesecake. (C'mon, I needed carbs for the next day's game!)

One of the more difficult things I had to learn early on was controlling my adrenaline output on game day, especially with night games. I hadn't played but one or two night games in my entire college career, so when I got to the Steelers, I didn't really understand how draining they could be if you didn't understand how to prepare. The mental aspect of the game is key to any player's success. I had learned early on about how to get into the "theater of the mind," from *Psycho-Cybernetics* by Maxwell Maltz. My first offensive line coach with the Steelers, Rollie Dotsch, used to call it mental gymnastics. Essentially it meant envisioning yourself running every play in the playbook against every defense. Powerful stuff.

It's my strong belief that it's physically impossible to prepare yourself to run every play against every defense, and every variation that can occur on each play, in practice. There simply isn't enough time, energy, or strength to do it correctly. So it comes down to a matter of the mind. You can run infinite plays, and infinite variations of each play, against each defense, all within the comfy confines of the theater of your mind. I got so good at it, I could "grab a bag of popcorn" mentally as I entered into the mindset that I needed.

The downside was that to get it right, you had to "experience" it in as much self-created Sensurround as possible. You needed to smell the air, hear the sounds, feel the clash as you hit, run through all of the audibles, make sure you could hear the quarterback's voice giving the snap count. All this comes with an accelerated heart rate that would get you pumped up, especially if you engaged some music in the background via headphones. I must say, I got pretty good at it.

What I hadn't learned at that point was how to do it while turning off the adrenaline. Adrenaline is a very precious commodity, especially game-day stuff. If you could bottle game-day adrenaline, you would put every energy drink out of business. Well, throughout the day, as I spent hour after hour mentally rehearsing the game, I was burning my storehouse of precious adrenaline. And because I was all jazzed up to play the Giants in my first professional opportunity, I never even got sleepy, much less took a nap.

When you have an eight o'clock kickoff, the pregame meal is around four o'clock. After the pregame meal, I would typically jump on the early bus and head to the stadium. And the skill-position guys (I use that term loosely) would follow on a bus that came to the stadium 60 to 90 minutes later than us beefeaters.

The first thing I screwed up in my first outing was taking the second bus. Since it was my first travel game, I didn't realize the importance of getting there early, getting my ankles taped, and getting out of the way of the veterans. And it was a rule back then that *everybody* had to have their ankles taped.

If I had any preconceptions about what it would be like in the pregame locker room before our game with the Giants, they were quickly crushed. In college the locker room was normally very somber and quiet, so I was shocked when I walked into this visitor's locker room. It was anything but quiet. In fact, I stopped walking halfway through in sheer amazement. Guys were moving about, yelling to each other, laughing, and talking far above the accepted norm that was my collegiate experience.

I wasn't ready for this.

In one corner, Terry Bradshaw was sitting wearing shorts, a T-shirt, and a Red Man cap, with a big stogie in his mouth. He was sitting at a card table with a few other guys. He wasn't going over the game plan, as I would have assumed, but laughing, telling jokes, and playing cards. It was vintage Bradshaw, as I would come to know.

Other players were smoking cigarettes, some were chewing Red Man tobacco, or Skoal and Copenhagen snuff. Guys were in various levels of dress. A television and some music were competing with the general din of noise of 50 to 60 people bustling in, around, and about the confines of the locker room. To me it was a totally alien atmosphere. I even saw "Mean" Joe Greene crack a smile, for crying out loud!

Well, if the locker room atmosphere wasn't what I had been expecting, taking the field was even more mind-blowing than any collegiate experience. I had actually played at the Meadowlands twice during my senior year at Syracuse. That year, the school was tearing down old Archbold Stadium and building the Carrier Dome, so we had to play all of our home games on the road. We played at the Meadowlands, Rich Stadium in Orchard Park, and once at Cornell University in Ithaca. Even against Penn State at the Meadowlands, it didn't feel like we'd come close to filling it like the Giants fans did that night. Nor had there been someone as ornery as Harry Carson awaiting me on the other side of the ball.

In warm-ups, I could feel my heart thundering like a runaway horse in the midst of a stampede. The crowd, the Giants, the scared-stiff, am-I-really-ready-for-this? feeling deep down inside made catching my second wind a challenge. After warm-ups, we went back to the locker room to wait for the callout to the sideline for the kickoff. The locker room that had been so loose and carefree just an hour ago was now humming with an undercurrent of electrical energy.

The seriousness of the team was all centered on winning. Winning was everything to Coach Noll. Not mostly everything; I mean *all* of everything. In practice, in play, preseason, regular season, or postseason, the only acceptable performance outcome was winning. There was no substitute. It's a Pittsburgh Steelers thing. Winning was so important to Coach Noll, you literally couldn't tell the difference in his pregame demeanor from the regular season to the postseason.

As a matter of historical fact, in the very same stadium, against the New York Giants in another preseason game later in the '80s, the starting offensive unit played the first quarter and a half. We then were taken out of the game and sat around for the rest of the first half, halftime, and the third quarter, all of us thinking we were done for the rest of the game. But you would never see a Chuck Noll team with guys taking their shoulder pads off during the game, thinking their night was over, unless they had been injured. Because the unexpected could always happen.

And it did on that night in Gotham City. Suddenly, with about 10 minutes or so left in the fourth quarter, our line coach, Ron Blackledge, came by and quietly urged us to "buckle up." There was tension in his voice that indicated what was going to happen, but it was also tinged with his disagreement. And he wasn't kidding.

"Chuck wants to win the game. You guys [the first-team offensive line] are going back in," Blackledge said. We were awash in disbelief. We had been sitting around, letting our mental game slide since coming out in the second quarter. And, most problematic for us older guys—Webby, Tunch, and me—we had gotten stiff as boards. There we were, playing in the fourth and last game of the preseason, relaxing in the fourth quarter, watching the Giants backups and campers playing their hearts out. There was a serious jolt of attitude adjustment needed. We went back in the game, and thankfully we were able to put together a touchdown drive. And we did it against a lot of guys who wouldn't be on the Giants roster—or any other in the NFL—the next week. Sure, we won, but it was a painful way to experience Coach Noll's "winning isn't everything, it's the only thing" mentality.

But that was years later. Back in my first game, I was sweating it out in the bowels of the Meadowlands, grinding through a can of snuff, and anticipating the high-voltage clash that was sure to come when I hit the field. As we waited in the visiting team's locker room, the electricity moving through my body began to dwindle. I felt like a drain had been opened in me, or like I had crested a mountain and was starting down the other side. I almost yawned! I doubled down, digging into my mental reserves, trying to draw upon energy that had been there in abundance earlier in the day. It was right then that I learned to nap the afternoons of night games. But right now I was needlessly burning precious fuel, fuel that would be needed to go almost three quarters my first time out as a pro.

It was not the time to have a self-help talk to overcome the doubts that were peppering me. I'd literally prepared my entire life for this. So why the self-doubt now? Thankfully, before there came a crisis of confidence—something I came to see nearly paralyze other rookies—Coach

Noll breezed into the locker room and took center stage. I heard "Everybody up!" as we came together. We took a knee, recited the Lord's Prayer, and made final preparations. There was a lump in my throat that felt like the size of my fist.

Go time was finally here, and everybody headed to the door. Then came the all-too-familiar herding of bodies bumping and banging against each other while walking through the tunnels to take the field. The roar of the crowd enveloped us. The fading light from the day intermixed with the huge lights hovering over the Meadowlands Complex. It all made for a surreal moment. For a brief flash I was teleported back to old War Memorial Stadium, where I saw my first professional football game (also a night game). That game had hooked me for life, and now it was my turn. I was about to experience my first real go as a professional football player. When people tell you that they've been waiting their whole life for a certain moment, I get exactly what they mean. I had told my mother as a seven-year-old boy that I intended to become a football player. Right here, right now, was the culmination of that promise, which God chose to grant me 15 years later.

As kickoff approached, I could barely contain myself. I was surrounded by great players and future legends. The Steelers had won their fourth Super Bowl the season before, and all of Pittsburgh was clamoring for number five; "one for the thumb" was the rallying cry.

Finally, the game began. The Giants ran the ball on first and second down. On third down, Phil Simms threw a quick out to a Giants wideout. The receiver's name escapes me, but Mel Blount's quick and decisive play will forever be etched into my consciousness. The receiver had caught the ball just a few steps from the sideline near the first-down sticks, where I had positioned myself after kickoff. Since I was on the punt-return team, I had made sure I was in the staging area and attending to what was happening on the field. Blount, in man coverage, swooped in with a fierceness I had never seen up close and personal before. Jumping the out cut, Mel closed on his prey. Like an eagle pouncing on a field mouse, he wrapped up the smaller receiver in his huge frame and *lifted* him up and over his hip, like a judo throw! Mel slammed the player headfirst into the hard artificial turf, dislodging both the ball and the receiver's mental faculties. (Remember, this was 1980, folks. A different era. Big hits like this were celebrated all over the league, not just in Pittsburgh.)

The receiver lay there, gradually coming to, trying to get to his feet but having little success. He was obviously stunned. Today he would have been ushered off to a sideline tent and immediately placed in the concussion protocol. Mel stood calmly nearby, hands on his hips, looking like the baddest man on the planet. I would come to learn it was simply his calling card. He was so physically dominant, the NFL permanently changed the rules of engagement for defensive backs because of him. I had a conversation with Mel years later, and he said, "Young D-backs point at me and say, 'There goes the guy who ruined it for us.'"

There was a timeout, and just before the Giants trainers got to their player, Mel simply unbuckled his chinstrap and walked to the sideline. No histrionics, no gyrating, no celebrating. Just a man getting his business done, and done at a level few would ever match. I'm sure my jaw was hanging open. I had heard about Mel, had seen him in action on TV and grown up hearing of his incredible exploits from Howard Cosell, "Dandy" Don Meredith, and others. And I had tangled a little with him myself at training camp, when I was trying to block him, but he had seemed more annoyed with my efforts than threatened.

Here, in living color, and in a sudden explosion of power, speed, and strength, I had witnessed with my own eyes what a Super Bowl champion, perennial Pro Bowler, All-Pro, and future Hall of Famer looked like up close. It was overpowering—better than advertised.

I don't remember much else about the game until I got the call to go in. I was surprised that it came with Bradshaw still at quarterback. That normally didn't happen in the preseason; nobody wants a rookie lining up next to them among a veteran group. I had played special teams early on in the game, so after blocking someone on the punt return, I stood in the Steelers huddle and waited for the rest of the offense to join me for the first play from scrimmage. I remember taking a deep breath, trying to compose myself, looking around, thinking that this was an accomplishment just to be here. I couldn't have known a year earlier, while on the field against Penn State, that I would be here again as a Pittsburgh Steeler against the New York Giants. Incredible.

Looking around the huddle, into the other players' eyes, feeling the drumbeat of the crowd, our quarterback called the play toss 32 trap, and we broke the huddle. I was practically hyperventilating at this point. Jogging to the line, I remember peeking to my right over to the area in which I would attempt to trap somebody. Whoever filled in the hole over the right tackle as I pulled, that would be the guy I would try to "earhole." Trapping is an unusual commitment to an unnatural concept. It's kind of like trying to run full speed into a parked car. It's just not for everybody.

My motor was running full steam. All sorts of craziness pinged through my mind as I listened to the snap count. I was at left guard for longtime starter and team captain Sam Davis. I lined up in the two-point stance prior to the quarterback setting us into the three-point, hand-in-the-turf stance everybody knows. I have always mentally practiced and associated the sound of a snap count with a gunshot, like a starter's pistol. Using that analogy helps me to really zoom in and focus on the quarterback's voice, to anticipate the snap count. Just as a good marksman will hold his breath during a respiratory pause prior to firing the gun so he doesn't move and cause himself to miss the target, I would anticipate the snap count. An offensive lineman's greatest weapon is the ability to properly utilize the snap count. We're talking mere heartbeats of an advantage here.

The ball was snapped and I remember exploding out of my stance, whipping my right elbow back and twisting my torso to the right. I pumped my left fist in front of me. I gained ground on my first step, the echo of Rollie Dotsch's coaching tips having been ingrained in my soul. Pulling to my right, I remember the flash points: Mike Webster's butt as he came off the ball, Steve Courson at right guard double-teaming with Webby, and right tackle Larry Brown pass-setting on George Martin. If Martin read pass and started rushing the passer, Larry would turn him out. If Martin "rammed," or went hard to the inside, then I would trap Martin and Larry would go up to the second level and get Carson.

The Giants were playing a classic 3-4 defense with three down linemen and four linebackers. Defensive end Martin read pass and started to bull-rush straight ahead. He was locked up with Brown. Now, if I saw that action, my job was to adjust my path and lead the running back up into the hole and block, most likely, Carson. One problem: I was so over-amped and fixated on destroying whoever appeared in my line of sight, I was like a heat-seeking missile. Sprinting at the top end of my RPM spectrum, nearly catatonic from frenziedness, I bore down on Martin, and subsequently my teammate Brown as well. I was so locked in on Martin's No. 75 jersey that I don't recall, to this day, seeing Larry at all.

I don't know what made Brown look to the inside. Maybe it was the look on Martin's face, a "look out!" as he viewed the car crash about to happen. Maybe it was a premonition to avoiding a season-ending injury. I don't know. All I know is at the snap of the ball, I must've sounded like a screaming banshee rolling out of control downhill. Exhaling buckets of air as I screamed my way toward the entangled bodies on the right side, I dropped my head just prior to impact, ready to impale George while never seeing Larry.

I would like to tell you that my first play from scrimmage was a huge success. Or at least a success. Or even a draw. That I mulched George Martin with a thunderous block, springing our running back for a touchdown run. Oh, to be a hero on your very first play as a pro. What the tape will tell you is that the guy I should have blocked, Harry Carson, read the trap, stepped up and closed the gap, and drilled our running back for little to no gain.

Meanwhile the overfrenzied rookie pulling guard launched himself at the tangled mass of George Martin and the still-unseen Larry Brown. The tape will show at some point that both combatants, probably hearing my insane screaming, looked inside and simultaneously jumped backward and away from each other, thus avoiding my futile attempt at wiping them out as I streaked in between them. Further video evidence will show that my hallowed first snap, my long-awaited, long-anticipated first play, ended with me spectacularly auguring myself into the Meadowlands turf, whiffing on everybody, teammates included. I hit face-first with a crash that had to have registered on the Richter scale. "Pitiful" is the only word that comes to mind.

"Did you get anybody?" Mike Webster asked as I wobbled back into the huddle.

"Nope," I simply said.

"Nope," Larry Brown echoed from his side of the huddle. "He missed."

CHAPTER 6

WORKING AS ONE

In football, there are certain fundamental truths. Relying on your instincts is crucial. The X's and O's look *oh so* different when they begin moving. And offensive lines that play together for a number of years have a massive advantage over lines that are revolving doors. When crunch time comes, knowing the man next to you, and the man a few doors down, can mean the difference between success and failure.

Of course, you learn this on the job, not in the classroom. One of the advantages of playing in the pre–free agency period was that a lot of offensive line units stayed together. As a result, the uniformity of becoming one mind, one fist with which to hammer the opponent, was much more of a thing back in the day. The Steelers linemen with whom I started playing—Jon Kolb, Ray Pinney, Mike Webster, Steve Courson, Larry Brown, Tunch Ilkin, Terry Long—were either longtime vets or guys who remained there for a large part of the 1980s. Although Pinney left for a brief stint in the USFL, he made his way back to Pittsburgh, to the cheers of Tunch and me.

We as vets developed an understanding of our teammates' playing characteristics and knew how our ability to group-think on each play gave us an advantage, even an ability to adjust on the fly in emergencies. Such as the day we played the Oilers in the Astrodome in 1987.

During the Oilers' heyday as perennial AFC Central contenders in the late 1970s through the 1980s, we as a group had to bunch tightly together in the huddle, helmet to helmet, just to hear the play call. The noise level there at that time was deafening. The Astrodome was called the Eighth Wonder of the World when it opened in 1965. It was the world's first indoor, air-conditioned, domed stadium, which, of course, suited me, because Houston is generally hot and humid for the majority of the NFL season. As an NFL rookie, I'd never played indoors, so my first time in Houston was a rather novel experience.

Built as a multipurpose facility, MLB's Houston Astros and the NFL's Houston Oilers both played their home games there. It was the stage for the infamous Battle of the Sexes tennis match in 1973, when Billie Jean King defeated Bobby Riggs. It was also the backdrop for Evel Knievel's record-setting motorcycle jump in 1971. Judy Garland, the Supremes, Elvis, Selena, and George Strait all performed there. The place even hosted indoor rodeos (which never helped the smell factor). Standing 18 stories high, it was intimidating from the outside. The turf inside the dome was the first rollout of what would become the bane of all knees, an artificial playing surface called Astroturf.

Smoke from the unfiltered cigarettes being puffed by the Steelers-hating fans who packed the dome accumulated as a haze over the undisputably worst playing surface in the NFL. Just how bad was it? They once replaced a four-by-eight-foot piece of turf with a four-by-eight-foot sheet of plywood. And I fell on the dadgum thing! I suppose it was nice of them, though, to paint it green. I'm sure from the upper reaches of the stands you couldn't tell the difference.

Oilers superfan Crazy George banged away furiously on his tom-tom, continually pushing the crowd to frenzied heights and raising the decibel level ever higher. Before the game, Crazy George came down to a front-row seat in the end zone where we went through our warm-ups and screamed at Mike Webster. It got to the point where Webby pointed at him and yelled, "I'd like to take that stupid drumstick and turn you into a human Popsicle!" You can only imagine how crazy the atmosphere was to get a reaction like that from Webster.

Our game there in 1987 was tight, and seesawed back and forth. Slowly we began to get our footing in the run game and found a rhythm. Having captured some of that mojo moving into the second half, we were on the hunt as we dialed up a drive and headed into Oilers territory. Facing a makeable third-and-short, we were right on the bubble of being able to run or pass. Having screamed out the play in the huddle just moments before, quarterback Mark Malone paused and warily surveyed Houston's defensive front before going under center. Standing behind

Steelers linemen (from left to right) Mike Webster, me, and Ray Pinney work as one to open a gaping hole for Franco Harris. Courtesy of the Pittsburgh Steelers

Mike Webster, Malone put his hands under center expecting Houston's defense to stem, shift, or show their hand prior to the snap.

The Oilers were in their base Okie 3-4 defense, with an inside linebacker lined up five yards deep over me. Suddenly, he walked up on my outside shoulder at the left guard position, and, by doing so, unknowingly had just drawn a bull's-eye on himself. He had just walked himself into the perfect alignment for a 93 tackle trap, and everybody on the offensive line knew it. It was one of the checks we had worked on all week.

Webster, crouched over the ball with those arms that looked as big as other people's legs, acted as the proverbial coach on the field and yelled to Malone that we needed to get out of the play we were in. Malone, hearing Webby and seeing the linebacker walk up, was on the same page with Coach Mike. And the trap play Mark checked into was a beauty, artfully designed by offensive coordinator Tom Moore for just this situation.

Across the board, all of us hogs were in our two-point stances, straining to hear Mark scream out the audible above the cacophony of the crowd. The Oilers countered with their own checks and added to the mayhem of the moment. With the play clock winding down and everybody on both sides of the line poised in launch mode at DEFCON 5, it looked more like a Wild West shootout than a football game. Players on both sides of the line of scrimmage were drawing in deep, tortured breaths. With muscles quivering, a sudden sneeze would've launched one gigantic, ballistic pig pile.

The trap play was hot. I didn't have to think it all through because it was part of my DNA at this point. The blocking rules for a linebacker walking up on my outside shoulder called for me initially to let him run through. I would fake a pass set on him in an attempt to occupy his vision and then block down to the inside on the backside linebacker, either comboing with Webster on the nose tackle or through a direct release to the back side. Tunch, coming from my right, would blindside the 'backer and Frankie Pollard would hit the hole, lickety-split. In the perfect world of my playbook, with the linebacker lined up on my outside shoulder, it was a walk-in.

Steeling my gaze, I began thinking to myself, *Stay right there, baby. Tunch is about to go bug zapper on you.* Indeed, Tunch Ilkin, pulling from his right tackle position, would have an opportunity to drop a slobberknocker of a hit on him. It was almost like stealing candy from a baby. That linebacker wouldn't even see him coming. I mean, they don't call it a trap play for nothing. The linebacker, staring intensely at Malone and nobody else as he stood over me, would get a free run right into the backfield. Pollard, our running back, would take the quick handoff from Malone and rip through the vacated spot after Tunch vaporized the 'backer.

However, just seconds before the snap of the ball, the linebacker suddenly moved from my left shoulder and into the gap between Webster and me. Trust me when I tell you he was tight to the line of scrimmage, so close he was practically in Malone's mustache. How he wasn't called offside I'll never know. The tackle trap, so perfect just two seconds before, was suddenly compromised by the linebacker jumping into the A gap. Suddenly he was positioned where he could hit Malone, Frankie, the handoff, or even all three before Tunch could get to him.

Schnikes. What do you do? The rules for an adjustment like that called for me to let the 'backer go; Malone would beat the hit and hand off the ball. But all of my *Lost in Space* robot warning bells were screaming, "Danger Will Robinson!" This guy was going to hit the handoff. I just knew it. So while the book says to let Tunch deal with him, my instincts were telling me that Pollard's health was at stake and that this was going to end worse for him than the coyote in a Road Runner cartoon.

The angry faces of Tunch, Malone, Tom Moore, and Chuck Noll passed through my mind—but so did the unconscious face of my running back. It was too late in the snap count to warn Tunch, and Webby was concentrating on the snap, so he was ignoring me. A mere slight inhale and two heartbeats before Iron Mike snapped the ball, I went rogue, broke the rules, and decided to take the linebacker in the gap.

This is where playing together over the years rocks. I knew that Tunch would trap the area or drill the first man past my butt, whether he was in the A or B gap. He could read it and adjust on the fly. But the margin for error was slim, and the potential for getting somebody killed was high. At the snap, without a word spoken between any of us, the line moved as one. I crushed the linebacker down to the inside. Ray Pinney, playing left tackle, pass-set and clubbed the defensive end outside. Webster, knowing I had no choice, blocked back on the nose tackle by himself. Terry Long, playing right guard, blocked back on the defensive end over Tunch. Tunch came screaming and nailed the next man in the hole. Pollard hit it for a big play.

Everything went like clockwork, and there was nobody more relieved than me. After all, had one thing gone wrong, Frankie Pollard wouldn't be speaking to me to this day. Would you, Frankie?

CHAPTER 7

CENTER OF ATTENTION

Training camp has its drudgeries, to be sure. Even for a broadcaster. As my longtime career in pro football moved into the realm of media, it wasn't all cakes and scones. Training camp could become rather mundane, especially after the really good action drills (such as Oklahoma or backs-on-backers) had either been retired from the game—like me—or relegated to a once- or twice-a-camp gladiatorial spectacle. The pressure-packed confrontation and demolition in those drills brings out the very best and worst of these fierce combatants seeking to stand out from the rest. The big bang theory of who just steamrolled whom naturally emerges from those of us among the blood-sport crowd looking to crown a winner, point to a loser, or just call it a draw.

The discerning fan who pays attention to less obvious characteristics can glean from the muddled collisions an insight into what might lay ahead for certain players. Such was my experience watching LeShawn Maurkice Pouncey begin to separate himself from the pretenders as a contender.

Maurkice played his college ball at Florida, was a member of a BCS National Championship team with the Gators, was recognized as a consensus All-American, and won the 2009 Rimington Trophy, awarded annually to the best college football center. He was drafted in the first round by the Steelers in 2010, and went on to play in 134 games for them in 10 seasons; he was a nine-time Pro Bowler, five-time All-Pro, and was named to the NFL 2010s All-Decade Team. He is the twin brother of another former NFL center, Mike Pouncey. But he was just another rookie in his first camp on this day.

The first day of camp is always a well-attended affair. At my rookie camp, the year after the fourth Lombardi Trophy had been won, there were 20,000 fans in attendance that first day—a huge crowd. But even after non-title-winning seasons, the crowds are large and raucous. Fans can spot the hot drill of the moment just as readily as the combatants, and the crowd jacks the intensity level up considerably. Add to that cacophony your peers, who are standing next to the coaches and just in front of the scouts and press guys. Every adventure and misadventure will be dissected, discussed, and then broken down on the internet the next day. Now, add a dash of the considerable alpha-male egos inherent in most players and you have a combustible cauldron that can bubble over at any time. In other words, fighting is a natural component of the drill, because winning it is a source of pride and a way to demonstrate where a player stands amid the pack of alpha males who are his teammates. You can't fake your way to alpha status; you gotta earn it.

And when one-on-one drills are happening at camp, you know you're really in the place to be when Mike Tomlin is also there supervising the action. Large and in charge, Tomlin's running commentary is appreciated by both players and outsiders. So this is where things get interesting. I wanted to get a good view of Pouncey's first one-on-one in a highly physical drill in which two opposing linemen square off for a pass rush. The defensive lineman has the edge because he doesn't have to go through his run reads; he just has to focus on timing the snap and beating the offensive lineman to get to the quarterback (who's generally played by a ball boy or the line coach).

What normally transpires with young guys, who may be caught up in the moment, is the desire to win at all costs, meaning the heck with technique. So some will do *anything* to win in the moment, which is exactly what not to do. Coaches want to see a player learn his technique and execute it properly. Doing whatever it takes to win may surface on game day, but you're never going to build your technique unless you consistently work on it, day by day. And the pass-rush drill is the perfect training ground for it; if you can do it in an isolated, heavily weighted one-on-one encounter, chances are you'll get it done on game day.

And here's where I was so impressed by Maurkice Pouncey. With all the pressure of being a rookie, a first-rounder, a guy competing to be a starter right away, there was a lot going on. The intensity of the moment can break you mentally, trust me. Yet there was Pouncey, called up for a mano a mano matchup with the Steelers' first-round draft pick from the previous year, defensive tackle Ziggy Hood. Now, Ziggy may not have had the sparkling career his draft status suggested, but there was no denying that he was a physical stud. (And, hey, he did ultimately spend 10 years in the league.)

I was fired up to see these two first-rounders square off. Both players took their respective places, eyeballing each other as they got into position. Hood aligned on the outside shoulder of Pouncey and at the snap of the ball crossed over to the inside in a ridiculously quick maneuver that caught Pouncey off guard. Hood came with the quick swim, or arm over, and beat the pants off the rookie.

Whoa! The catcalls, hooting, and hollering came from the fans. The players jeered or cheered, depending on whether they wore black for offense or gold for defense. The coaches immediately descended on the two combatants to verbally critique what they had just seen. I could see Pouncey getting his mojo revved up, refusing to acknowledge what had happened. He gazed at Hood with a searing look that spelled *r-e-m-a-t-c-h*. I would come to know this look over the years as I patrolled the sideline in my broadcasting duties. When Pouncey started to vibrate like that, somebody was going to pay.

Something was brewing in Pouncey's mind, and it's in these moments—these terse, in-between-the-combat moments—that players either regroup and shine, or they fold like a cheap card table and retreat internally, maybe even externally. I mean, after some bad reps, I've seen whupped guys suddenly need a new shoestring. Or maybe experience an unexpected cramp. Anything to take themselves out of the rep cycle.

Obviously, there's no such shrinkage in Pouncey. Tomlin, of course, called for the rematch, and the noise level rose accordingly. You could feel the Latrobe heat index rise as Pouncey, seemingly oblivious to the verbal storm that had assailed him, lined up for a second go with Hood. I

Maurkice Pouncey continued the Steelers' tradition of great centers. My wingmate Mike Webster, pictured here snapping to Terry Bradshaw, was another. Courtesy of the Pittsburgh Steelers

remember leaning over to Tunch Ilkin and asking, "Does Pouncey try to win this at all costs or does he stick with his technique?" Chalooch (as we called Tunch) nodded in agreement, and we both focused on Pouncey.

We didn't have to wait long for an answer. When the ball was snapped, Pouncey set perfectly, making sure not to overset the way he had the first time. With very quick hands and a good, solid punch, Pouncey executed a perfect pass-pro one-on-one, stuffing Ziggy on the rematch. It was totally clean.

I don't remember if they had a third go-round or if they ended the day in a draw, but what I saw in that moment of rematching was enough to convince me that Pouncey was going to be a player of consequence. Now, who could've known the greatness that lay ahead for Pouncey? I certainly didn't. But this I did know: With all the pressure that comes with being a first-round draft pick, with being inserted into the starting lineup almost from day one, getting smoked in his first live go at camp in front of everybody, the young buck did not rattle. He was confident in his skill and technique and didn't fold to the pressure of his ego. He simply demonstrated better technique, skill, and that killer's edge we all came to know.

I have had the great privilege of watching every one of Maurkice Pouncey's 134 regular-season games (not to mention his playoff games) from the sideline. I also had the privilege to line up next to the late, great Mike Webster for eight years. And I can tell you that along with Dermontti Dawson, with whom I played for a couple of years, the Steelers have had three of the greatest centers to ever play the game.

Two of those greats are already in the Hall of Fame. The third one, LeShawn Maurkice Pouncey, in my opinion, is simply biding his time until he gets that gold jacket. And the first indicator of that greatness was, to me, born during a simple one-on-one drill at St. Vincent College.

CHAPTER 8

THE HAMMER

To be honest, I was licking my lips. No, it wasn't Taco Tuesday at the lunch truck. I don't think lunch trucks even existed back on this day. I was just feeling a little excited, a little "froggy" about what was coming next. And, hey, I couldn't help but feel confident. I had been doing well and holding my own in the first couple weeks of my rookie training camp with the Steelers.

An inner smile creased my consciousness as I took a look at the lineup I was facing in a half-line drill. It was a drill that emphasized the running game, played versus half of the defense. All the running plays had to be aimed at the right side of the offense, left side of the defense. Drafted out of a run-first, run-last, run-whenever-you-had-the-freakin'-ball offense at Syracuse University, I was built for this drill. I mean, once, against NC State, we ran the ball 55 times. A pass play had been called, but we audibled out of that at the line to a rush play. I felt I might be able to kick a little butt in a drill like this one.

So there I was at left guard on a 36 trap, pulling to my right, running a trap play that would be right off the butt of the right tackle and the tight end, who would be working on a double-team block on the defensive end to that side. Whoever showed up in the six hole would be mine as I pulled down the line of scrimmage. When you trap an end or a linebacker in a 4-3 defensive configuration coming from the left guard position, it's several yards of turning and sprinting, unless the end man on the line of scrimmage closes the trap. Then, instead of a *thwap!* like when you clobber a fly on the kitchen counter, the defense is taught to "trap the trapper." It then turns into a high-intensity human demolition derby. Whether the end man on the line closes the trap or not, the sudden stop at the end of the play feels like running into a parked car wearing a helmet and chin strap.

When you're a rookie, there are always ups and downs at that first training camp. Besides having to navigate a multitude of matchups against future Hall of Famers, there's your coach, demanding that you understand the *theory* of each play. Understand what you're trying to show to the defense by formation. Understand how the defense would react to said formation. Understand what motion on a play did to the defense. Understand what motion and a shift in the defense would do to the play. Sheesh, that's a whole lotta understanding going on. I just wanted to hit somebody. But I quickly learned that engaging in mental gymnastics, visualizing the plays with defensive scenarios, would become a huge part of my daily ritual.

Every day we were challenged on the practice field. *Every. Single. Day.* Mentally and physically. And for the first couple of weeks, it was twice a day. And then we had to do it in the classroom as well, whether it was the installation of new plays or the ever-entertaining film review sessions, where we bottom-feeder rookies were the constant fodder for group enjoyment. And every day you had to respond. Bad days and poor performances weren't well tolerated. As the saying goes, "Get good or get gone."

So I stood in the huddle and reviewed the trap play in my head. *Pull tight to the line. Make sure to get up into the offensive line. Anticipate the right side of the line blowing back the defensive line to some degree. The DE will get double-teamed and the outside linebacker will most likely squeeze down while jamming the TE to his inside. And then I have to be ready for whatever gold defensive jersey pops out to close the trap.*

I was all too aware of the individuals who comprised the murderer's row on the half of the defense we were facing. There was "Mean" Joe Greene, L. C. Greenwood, Jack "Splat" Lambert, and the Hammer, Jack Ham. I eyeballed the Hammer from across the line of scrimmage as we stood in the huddle.

Ham was a key element in an exceptionally strong left side of the Pittsburgh defense during the team's Super Bowl years. Drafted in 1971 out of Penn State, he was named All-AFC in 1973 and became an All-Pro the next six consecutive seasons. *Football News* named him

Defensive Player of the Year in 1975. He was named to eight straight Pro Bowls. Of course I'd watched the exploits of the great Jack Ham while growing up. I had deep respect for his ability. But I also thought that by now, in his 10th year, I had an opportunity. I mean, if you only saw his gray beard, even *you* might think you had a chance. I looked over at him, practically licking my lips. Whipping a future Hall of Famer by crushing him in a half-line drill was a sure way to get noticed. And I intended to get noticed.

At the snap of the ball, I exploded out of my stance. Pulling to my right, I whipped my right arm back in a shoulder-turning maneuver I had practiced seemingly all my life. I was running down the line of scrimmage like a runaway train toward the six hole, filled with bad intentions and thoughts of self-aggrandizement after blowing up the great Hammer. I made sure I gained ground up the field, to be sure, because there's no way I would allow leakage by taking a bad angle and messing up the play. I felt like a lion on the hunt, ready to kill when the prey showed itself.

It was at about this point that the whole "hunting down my prey" thing went sideways. Literally. Nobody showed as I pulled and approached the end of the line. Just as I arrived at the six hole, there was a flash, a bang, and a bounce—in that order—and from where Jack Ham came, to this day, I do not know.

The flash was the incredible closing speed with which the Hammer suddenly appeared in my face. Or more to the point, my inside shoulder. The bang occurred nearly simultaneously with the flash, and it was truly, to that point in my career, the hardest I had been hit in my life. The bounce came after I hit the dirt. I was left to feel as if all of my innards were now mulchified. And the pain I was experiencing had nothing to do with my ego taking a dirt beatdown. Oh, yeah. The pain was real. So was the dirt I spit out of my mouth. I rolled over and staggered to my feet, not sure into what reality I had just checked. I just couldn't get over how hard Jack had hit me.

The guy was close to 50 pounds lighter than me, a decade older than me, and I was way stronger than he was. *Way* stronger. It was that he appeared from nowhere, too. I didn't even see him until it was too late. He made me look like a rocket ship launching from Cape Canaveral. And I mean to tell you, he launched me and I was flying sideways before I splatted.

After I shook the shooting stars from my noggin, I tried to focus on my line coach, Rollie Dotsch, who immediately commenced to face-melt me on what a horse-crap blocking attempt that was. After a moment or two of taking in Rollie's wrath, I gathered what little pride I had left and walked back to the huddle. The defense was now woofing it up, and there was a considerable rise in the volume of banter and trash-talking going on between the O-Line and D-Line. Defensive line coach George Perles was verbally jousting with Rollie at this point—poking the bear, if you will, over how the defense blew up the play in general, and me in particular.

Before I got back to the huddle, though, I glanced over at the defense, and there stood the Hammer with a grin on his face. Over and over, in my head, I'm thinking, *I'm 50 pounds heavier, way stronger, and way younger. And...I...just got destroyed...by a legend.* And...well...that's why they call them legends.

Suddenly it dawned on me: I wasn't in Kansas, or even Syracuse. Nope. No, I wasn't.

CHAPTER 9

OFF TO SEE THE WIZARD

One of the horrors of doing training camp in extreme heat is dehydration. That, of course, can lead to cramping. Otherwise known as "locking up," it's something that, for me, became a rather accepted norm, the cost of doing business in 80-, 90-degree heat and high humidity. Guys from the South and warm-weather areas don't seem to be much affected. Me, having lived and played ball all my life in the Northeast and only occasionally running into the heat and humidity conditions that can endanger your life? I had *muchas problemas* with it.

Lockup is brutal. It feels like your muscles all melt down completely and then the cramps get so bad it feels like your muscles are trying to tear off your bones. I've been told that once you experience the full phenomenon, you are susceptible to more. I'm no doctor, but that was sure true

Staving off dehydration and cramping was just a part of summer football. Courtesy of the Pittsburgh Steelers

for me. No doubt football has evolved over the last century-plus. Water breaks were unheard of for those guys who used to fold up their leather helmets and put them in their back pockets after practice. Coaches were legendary for not letting their troops swill H_2O. Fortunately, I came along in the era of water breaks and Gatorade. And believe me, when Gatorade came out with that lemon/lime mix in the late '70s, I gulped that stuff like it was liquid gold.

Heat exhaustion, cramping up, and related risks didn't come to the forefront until former Minnesota Vikings offensive tackle Korey Stringer passed away in 2001. Korey, a 27-year-old Pro Bowler and six-year veteran, died from complications from heat stroke during training camp in Mankato, Minnesota. Prior to his death, cramps, heat exhaustion, and heat stroke hadn't really been a priority for the medicos.

Of course, I had cramped up before. In college I had a run-in with heat exhaustion, but I didn't go into the total debilitating mode of full-body cramping. Maybe a thigh here, a triceps or pectoral quiver there, but nothing more. Ultimately I would become familiar with the telltale signs. And I'm here to tell you that if you did "vapor lock," you were about to set off on an excursion into the twilight zone of pain tolerance. Once I felt a couple of twinges, or the muscles began to tweak and jump or move of their own accord, I was scrambling for a trainer. I knew what was coming.

In the early 1980s, I had not mastered the art of rehydrating properly after practice or games. Later on, in my wizened years, I finally understood that rehydrating, for me, meant drinking an enormous amount of fluid—not a little, not a lot, but a gallon a night before bed. But back then, because I was drinking as much as other guys around me, I believed I was good to go. Yet I continued to experience brushes with cramping, and they seemed to get a little worse with each episode. It might start in the calves, work its way up to my thighs, hammies, and continue moving northward...until I eventually found myself in the hospital.

Today's trainers will hook you up to an IV that will speed the rehydrating process and preempt the trip altogether. But not back then. I actually spent a couple of nights in Latrobe Area Hospital. My cramping had almost become a laughing matter. In fact, Coach Noll once said jokingly, in front of the team, that my room at the hospital was all set.

Life in a Chuck Noll training camp consisted of rising, hitting someone, conditioning, hitting someone again, then sitting in infernal meetings until your eyes rolled back into your head. Then wash, rinse, repeat. You're constantly beat up, tired, and cranky. And cranky was how I began an argument with Tunch one day, stating that the heart was not a muscle but a part of the cardiovascular system. Little did I know I was going to have an opportunity to back up my argument soon.

After the second of two practices the next day, I began to feel a little bit of the twinges and tweaks that foretold incoming pain. Tunch and I started back up into our argument. My telltale signs of cramping seemed to lessen as I gulped post-practice Gatorade. They abated almost entirely, so it felt like time to roll on to the dining hall for chow.

Tunch and I started out of the locker room and slowly made our way toward the cafeteria. Those blessed women of St. Vincent College, the nuns, were cooking, so we weren't in a great hurry. (More on that some other time.) As we rounded the corner of a building and started on the gentle uphill to the cafeteria, my calf cramped. Out of nowhere, it just started to lock up. I tried to stretch it a little, but it persisted. All of a sudden the cramps moved to my quads—and I mean in a big way. First one thigh, then the other. I tried to stretch the one leg, and the muscle would release, only to have the other thigh muscle suddenly flex so hard it was excruciating. Trying to lean back to relax the front of my thighs, my hamstrings suddenly flexed out with that off-the-bone feeling. Sweat broke out on my forehead as I realized that a total body cramp was coming.

Suddenly unable to walk, or even move forward, I groaned as I inadvertently sank to the ground in pain, finding the only bit of grass along the way for a shred of comfort. Tunch stood over me with a curious look on his face. The cramps now had continued their painful march upward, fully engaging my abdominal muscles and causing me to try to lean backward to relieve the pain of my abs. Once they released, my lower back suddenly began locking up. Couple this with my thighs and my hammies alternating bolts of pain, and you can see my dilemma.

Gasping from the pain, I pushed my upper body slightly off the ground and immediately felt my pectoral muscles join in the chorus of pain, sending me crumpling back to the ground. Looking up at Tunch, I said with a clenched jaw, which was starting to cramp as well, "Do something!"

He didn't move. He said, "I am. We're about to find out who's right and who's wrong." He loves to be right. What can I say? At this point the pain became surreal. Everyone—students on campus, players, and otherwise—made wide berths around us. Writhing on the ground, sweating profusely, I yelped to Tunch, "Get a trainer!"

At this point I can't tell you if Tunch got our head trainer; Ralph Berlin, the assistant; or if one dropped from the sky. I didn't care. All I knew was that help was on the way. When you're in a world of hurt, time passes very slowly. And believe me, it did. Faces peered at me. People were talking, but I can't say who was there. I know that one of the trainers eventually arrived because at some point I became aware of a vehicle pulling up. Somebody said "hospital," and though I hate going to the hospital, I was in such pain that I was more than ready to go. I knew from past experience that despite what I was feeling now, it would only get worse.

So yes! An ambulance! Sweet mother of pearl, I could almost anticipate the relief.

Soon there were three or four people around me, each grabbing a limb and lifting me from the ground in a strained manner. Now somebody was counting to three, and after a slight swing forward, then backward, I was rocketed headfirst into the back end of a smelly old carpet van. I partially ricocheted off the rear bumper. Not even an ambulance? You've got to be kidding me.

It turned out that Robin Cole, a veteran linebacker, had locked up and been taken away in an ambulance sometime just prior to me. Seniority has its privileges, so the carpet van was the only available mode of transportation. No doctor, no EMTs, no medical personnel, not even a trainer came along for the ride with me. We were either that low on medical personnel or I was that expendable. (I believe it was more of the latter.)

As I lay on my back, alternating body positions to try to relieve whatever was currently trying to tear off the bone, through the pain I heard a young voice call back to me. It said, "Don't worry, Wolf. I know a shortcut." That voice was the kiss of death, to be sure. It was Dan Rooney Jr., Dan Rooney's teenage son, and he had *just* gotten his license.

We roared out of St. Vincent for the hospital as the cramps moved ever upward. I had to adjust my head position, trying to relieve the cramp currently in my neck, as Danny roared around some of the curves on campus. The pain rolled on, escalating for longer spasms. The relief never arrived, it just subsided ever so slightly. The ride, which should have only been 12 to 15 minutes in an ambulance, felt much longer. Lying in the back, unable to raise myself up because of the cramps shooting from one spot to another, I had no idea where we were. Until, coming out of yet another muscular spasm, I suddenly noticed that we weren't moving.

I began yelling at Danny. The poor guy became the focal point of my pain and anger. I asked him what in the world he was doing sitting at a light or a stop sign. I presumed we were in downtown Latrobe at this point. I rolled over onto my side and pushed upward. I could just glimpse corn from the side window.

Corn? What? Corn? Like cornstalks? Are you kidding me? Nope. Rows and rows of corn. I mean we were in the middle of a cornfield. Danny began to stammer at this point, unsure which way to go. He was lost. In a cornfield. Behind St. Vincent College. So much for the shortcut.

Another wave of pain cascaded through my body, and my forearms balled up so badly that my hands curled into claws. I hissed through teeth that were apparently trying to cement themselves together, “Danny, if I could uncurl my hands and reach you, I’d kill you!”

As if the threat had spurred him on, Danny chose a direction and hit the gas. He must have chosen well, or got a little divine inspiration at that moment, because we didn’t stop until we arrived at the hospital. I don’t know how Danny finally got the directions right. I don’t care if he had an epiphany or if a UFO scooped us up and dropped us off. All I knew was relief was here in the form of a wheelchair and nurses.

The back doors of the van swung open, the wheelchair was positioned, and I rolled to my side. I could feel hands pulling me to my feet. I spasmodically herked and jerked in pain as I was guided to the chair and strapped in. A trauma nurse jammed a needle into my arm, and pain I’d never experienced before (or since) racked my entire body, as first one part and then another went rogue. With my long hair and beard, and me almost foaming at the mouth at this point, I must’ve looked like someone more in need of a straitjacket and rubber room than an IV.

I was wheeled into the emergency room, where I was stuck with another needle. By the time I was lifted onto a bed, things were quieting down in my pain-racked nervous system. Oh yeah, they were slowing down. The spasmodic jerks began to subside. Slowly the muscles began to relax, and then relax some more. Oh yeah…

A little later, I became aware of music playing in the background. I’m not sure if it was playing in the emergency room or playing in my head, but I do know that I was beginning to float. It was almost as if I was having an out-of-body experience. Overjoyed at the absolute lack of pain, feeling moment by moment that pain-free high from the muscle relaxer/painkiller combo, I gradually became attuned to my surroundings.

Next to me, on another bed in the ER, was Robin Cole, my teammate who had the nice ambulance ride to the hospital, who didn't get lost in a cornfield, and who didn't need a straitjacket. Robin was rubbing his head and moaning a little. Hmmm, maybe he hadn't gotten the secret sauce that I did, because I was feeling no pain at this point whatsoever.

Robin's groan caught the attention of one of the nurses. She came to his side and asked if he was in pain and needed more of the secret sauce they had given him earlier. I don't think she actually used the term "secret sauce," but at this point I was pretty much having a conversation with Dorothy, the flying monkeys, and the Wizard of Oz himself (who looked a lot like Apollo 11 astronaut Buzz Aldrin, by the way).

Over the chatter of the flying monkeys, I heard Robin saying, "No, no, no, I hate that stuff." I remember squinting, trying to focus on the nice lady in white—or Dorothy, or whatever her name was. My foggy brain was trying to make sense out of a guy who didn't want this magical stuff that took away all cramps and pain, and basically made you float through Oz.

"I'll take it!" I blurted out. Rebuffed, I returned to my floating state of semi-awareness. I remember the doctor making his way toward me. Before he could even say anything, I asked the doc if he had any Pink Floyd. "Dark Side of the Moon! *Play the B side, baby!*"

The doctor gave the nurses instructions to have me cut off. So, I said goodbye to Robin and drifted off to the dark side of the moon myself, chatting up Buzz Aldrin and floating into that beautiful, sweet nothingness where pain doesn't follow.

CHAPTER 10

SAYING GOODBYE TO CHUCK

I think I'm pretty much like everybody else when it comes to funerals. It's a tough time, especially when the person being laid to rest is someone who has played a significant role in your life. So it was with a heavy heart and slow-footed approach to the funeral home my wife, Faith, and I went on that very sad day to pay our last respects to the Noll family and the man who had changed the arc, range, and trajectory of my life: former Steelers head coach Chuck Noll.

The large viewing area in the funeral home loomed as a soft backdrop to the gathering of former Steelers players, coaches, and front office personnel; Mr. and Mrs. Rooney and family; as well as the league officials who had gathered to say goodbye and pay their last respects to a man who had touched so many lives. Fidgeting with my tie, as I am wont to do in uncomfortable situations, I coughed and glanced around the room while taking in the moment. I gripped my wife's hand a little tighter, cleared my throat, and chastised myself for not having the foresight to bring a handkerchief.

My eyes drifted from Noll family members to Tunch Ilkin and his wife, to Roger Goodell, to others, and then settled on Joe Greene, the man who had kick-started a Steelers franchise that came to define the word *dynasty*. Joe was, as you would expect given the circumstances, respectfully quiet, withdrawn even. The customary smoldering aura that generally precedes him into each and every room was now gone like a campfire doused on a rainy night. Joe stood to my left and Tunch to my right as I rounded out a rough circle of those who had had the good fortune to have their lives touched by Charles Henry Noll.

I couldn't help but look at Joe the way I've always looked at him; he's always been larger than life to me. The samurai say that the window into a man's soul lies in his eyes—and if you've ever been on the wrong side of a glare from Joe Greene, you know that to be true. But it was in those very eyes that I saw such as I've never seen before in Mean Joe. I saw pure, unadulterated grief so deeply profound that words are incapable of expressing the depths of pain he was feeling. In that moment I saw the enormity of what Coach Noll had meant him.

Memories, reflection, and introspection during a period of mourning are natural by-products of grief. It was then, as I stood in Joe's shadow, that I began to reflect on my own interactions with Coach. He had influenced my life, and my outlook in general. He was the greatest coach in the history of the NFL, a man who personally shunned the spotlight but still walked in it wherever he went. Whether it was the first time I saw him or the last, it was always a time to remember, because you were always learning something in the time you spent with Chuck Noll.

Standing there adjusting, readjusting, and then finally waving the white flag of surrender to my rebellious tie, I talked, pretended to listen, and then just drifted away, slowly fading back to the first meeting I had with Chuck—when he traveled to Syracuse University to work me out before the draft in the spring of 1980. *Nervous* doesn't even begin to describe the churning in my gullet as I shook hands with Chuck Noll for the first time. He was, as he always would be, just himself. Coach was comfortable in his own skin, whether he was coaching, directing a symphony orchestra at training camp, discussing flying a plane, captaining a ship, dining on French cuisine, or elaborating on the characteristics of fine wines. I can truthfully say that I was in a state of awe when I first met him. And of course, as you already know, I ended up punching him right in the mouth that day.

Oh, tie, you're really starting to piss me off.

But my mind made a quick snapback the way Coach did that day, as he stood there wiping the blood off his mouth with his sleeve. A slow smile crept over his face, and the teacher in him told me it was all right. "Now *that's* a punch," he said. I absentmindedly chuckled to myself, and my wife shot me a curious look. But my cherished memories began spilling out, one after another. Chuck spotting Ray Pinney and the can of silicone spray, Chuck telling Jerry Glanville to meet him out in the parking lot outside the Astrodome, Coach and the pool ingredients, one of his many in-depth stories whose meaning we couldn't seem to grasp.

Coach was always big on teaching, and one topic he harped upon most dealt with learning to be a pro, and much of that dealt with pain and injury. "There's a difference between pain and injury," he would often lecture us. Yes, there was. And it was amazing how, with just a single look from Coach, you might experience the healing of an injury that only moments before you had thought would keep you out of practice. It sure worked on me.

In the mid-to-latter portion of my career, after being an established starter for several years, I pulled my groin in a game against the Bills. My left leg was black and blue, swollen two and a half inches larger than my right. I had gutted it out during the following week, through the Wednesday and Thursday practices, but with another game coming up, I felt I needed a break. I entered the training room and jumped up on the taping table, feeling a bit disgruntled and unappreciated on a Friday morning while getting ready for practice. Tunch and several others were already getting their ankles done up, and I said determinedly to the Turk, "I've got to have a day off. You know what? I'm telling Chuck I need to rest this thing. No way he's gonna make me practice today. I mean it!"

Tunch, always the instigator, laughed and then went straight to the heart of the matter as the rest of the training room listened in. "Sure, go ahead. I think you're entitled to a day off. Louis Lipps got time off for his hammy. Just tell Chuck you're hurting and you can't go. I dare you! No, I *double-dog* dare you!"

Looking at the rest of the room—which now, with Tunch chortling away, found themselves in on it—I loudly reiterated to Tunch, trainer Ralph Berlin, and anyone else listening that I would be taking the day off.

Hear me now and believe me later when I tell you there were a lot of doubters in that training room. With all the boldness of an idiot sawing off the very tree limb upon which he sat, I repeated yet again my determination to take off the padded practice scheduled for that afternoon.

You wouldn't believe it unless you had been there. Not 10 seconds later, as if all of this had been orchestrated and carried out on cue without my knowledge, right after that second public declaration of defiance, in walked Chuck. As Coach passed by the front of the taping table, he paused, turned, looked at me, and said, "Wolf, how's the leg?"

My head froze up like a block of ice. I tried to remember my reasons for not practicing. A clammy sweat suddenly broke out on my forehead, like I had a fever. In my mind, I was stating my case defiantly, like a teenager standing up to an unrighteous parental authority. In reality, what came out of my mouth was entirely a different matter. In the midst of having an out-of-body experience, I suddenly blurted out, "Great, Coach, I'm ready to go!"

"Good," he said as he whisked out of the training room and into the locker room. You can only imagine the grief I took and the gales of laughter that erupted in the training room after Chuck made his exit. And, yes, I *did* practice that day.

A tap on the arm from Faith startled me back to the present, to the last time I would see Coach. Even though we were beginning to move forward in the line to pay our last respects, I couldn't shake the vestiges of one more trip down memory lane. It was during the 75th anniversary of the Pittsburgh Steelers, and Chuck was being honored before a game at Heinz Field. I was standing ringside, as sideline analyst, during the ceremony, enjoying every minute as the man who had changed my life stood before the thunderous applause that washed over Heinz Field like an aural tsunami.

As I watched Chuck slowly walk to the sideline with his wonderful wife, Marianne, at his side, as she had been for virtually all of his life, I found myself needing to see him once more. I dodged between a number of people and came alongside Chuck. I extended my hand and bent over and said, "Coach, it's me, Craig Wolfley."

The handshake brought me close to Coach, virtually shoulder to shoulder. He looked at me and smiled. He said, "I know who you are," with such kindness that I was touched. With eyes that seemed to smile much broader at this moment than any I remember as a player, he smiled and with a slight chuckle said, "I see you've gotten into your life's work."

Indeed.

The pure pleasure of having Coach smile on me one more time leaves me feeling forever grateful for my time spent with Chuck Noll. He didn't just make me a better football player; he made me a better man.

CHAPTER 11

A MAJOR LEAGUE GAFFE

It's funny how you can watch someone else pull a boneheaded move and think to yourself, *How could you do that? I'd* never *do something that stupid.*

Oooh, baby, you wanna talk about a screwup? Sheesh. Look, I've been to loads of speaking engagements and meet-and-greets, and emceed a fairly sizeable number of charity and sports banquets over the last 30 to 40 years. And yes, in full disclosure, I have had some serious brain dysfunctions and delivered malaprops and unfunny jokes at crucial moments myself. I know what it's like to bomb on a stage.

Many years ago, while watching the evening news one night, I heard then-VP Joe Biden make what seemed like the gaffe of all gaffes while, at a campaign rally, he told Missouri state senator Chuck Graham to stand up. Graham was confined to a wheelchair. "What am I talking about?" Biden soon said. "I'll tell you what, you're making everybody else stand up, though, pal."

The replay was widely publicized. *Yeah*, I thought, *what a gaffe that was*! I mean, how in the world could you mess *that* up? I was incredulous...right up until I had my own boneheaded moment.

What's cool about the public-speaking realm are the different venues where you can find yourself speaking—to big crowds, little crowds, and all sizes in between. And among them, there are many different types of crowds. I thought I had been in front of some really boisterous, loud, and raw crowds over the course of my speaking career. And then came the elk hunters. Now, they were something else altogether. I had been contracted to appear, tell some stories, and do a meet-and-greet afterward. Usually meet-and-greets are an awesome time. Meeting Steelers fans always makes for a fun night, and I always hope I can provide them some entertainment in return and not get booed out of the joint.

So when I found out it was the Elk Hunters Association gig, I gotta tell you, I was looking forward to it. I was curious to see what they were all about. They were having a convention and dinner at a hotel north of

Speaking at the For Men Only conference in 2014.

Pittsburgh, and I had received a call to entertain the troops, as it were, for the evening. They were, let's just say, a wildly interactive group, who quite obviously enjoyed football stories, laughing, and in general having a good time.

There were some vendors present, displaying their products, selling hunting equipment, hunting trips, and all kinds of cool guy stuff. And they had various raffles and 50/50 drawings going on as well. And the adult libations had been flowing. Voices kept getting louder, guys got a little rowdier, and with some 500 or so elk hunters in the house, I was eager to spin a few tales and commence having fun after dinner.

So I got up and did my dog-and-pony act, told a few Tunch Ilkin stories, talked about the Steelers, and generally kept everything between the white lines. Nothing controversial, nothing pushing the edge, just general fun. Apparently, things went well enough that I didn't have to make a hasty exit. It was a very enthusiastic, well-lubed group that laughed and cheered at anything I said, whether it made sense to them or not. They were the type of crowd you'd love to entertain anytime. Comedian Billy Crystal used to say, "I just need a new audience every seven minutes." Well, these were the guys you'd love to keep rotating in. Elk hunters rock.

After my bit was over, they began doing raffles and 50/50 drawings. Well, apparently, someone didn't mix up or shuffle the ticket numbers to everybody's satisfaction, so I was called upon to be an impartial ticket puller. I mixed up the tickets, got elbow-deep in a big bowl of them, and drew one. After pulling the ticket, I announced the winner, and this person won to everybody's satisfaction. So now, because I had made the crowd happy, I had to stay there pulling tickets because I was viewed as a neutral ticket puller. After a few more moderate successes, the bigger raffle ticket gifts were gone and the crowd began to cluster into their own little fiefdoms. Conversations became centralized among their own personal roundtables, with the elk hunters regaling each other with their hunting exploits and heroic tales. But I was still charged with finishing off the remaining ticket prizes.

I pulled a raffle ticket and called the number. Nothing. At this point, I began losing the crowd. They were pretty much laughed out. I repeated the number, got a few semicurious looks, but not too many of them were tuning in. I repeated the number again, and nobody even glanced up from any of the conversations.

Feeling a little frustrated, and a little foolish because nobody was paying attention, I tried once more, booming my voice into the microphone. A group of guys near the center of the room that I hadn't noticed moments before waved at me, and I was told to cool my jets. They were crowding around a table, all bunched together, so I couldn't see what the heck was going on. Somebody standing on the outskirts of the crowded roundtable motioned toward somebody sitting there, so I bellowed, "If you've got the winning ticket, stand up, will you? There are so many guys I can't see you!"

Suddenly things quieted down and eyes snapped around to me all at once. Dumbfounded, I looked at the guys at the table, who were now staring at me. "Just stand up!" I said.

All at once the table exploded in laughter, as bawdy and raucous as you could imagine, and the guy standing at the table shouted out, "He would stand up, but he can't! He's in a wheelchair!"

That's when I realized I was a 300-pound Joe Biden. Oh man, I don't think I've ever apologized more, or was heckled louder, or heard more laughter over a gaffe than I did at that moment. But graciously, nobody laughed longer, harder, or was more wonderfully forgiving than the man in the wheelchair. Gotta love elk hunters.

CHAPTER 12
BAD RAD

Bad Rad. The tone accompanying the words rocked me more than just the mere mention of the man's nickname.

I was a few weeks into my first Steelers training camp at St. Vincent College, and I was having a typical rookie-to-mentor conversation with legendary Steelers center of the '70s Super Bowl years, Mike Webster. I had been talking to Mike about Rollie Dotsch, the offensive line coach when Tunch Ilkin and I were still bright-eyed and bushy-tailed rookies in 1980.

Of the first 16 days of training camp, 14 came complete with full pads and full-contact two-a-days amid fights, brutal conditioning runs, 90-plus heat and humidity, non-air-conditioned dorms, and suspect chow. The spartan existence of a Chuck Noll training camp had already lost bodies to injury, along with the occasional Bermuda Triangle victim. It wasn't unusual back then for a player to decide in the middle of the night that training camp wasn't for them; they just disappeared.

The conversation with Mike was about how tough Chuck was, how hard and unforgiving Rollie was, and how training camp life in general just sucked. That's when Webbie brought up Bad Rad—Dan Radakovich, the Steelers' O-line coach from 1974 to 1977. Basically, Mike made the case that Rollie was a walk in the park compared to Radakovich. Mike spoke his name with a tone of reverence, while laughing his way through physically exhaustive memories and the idiosyncrasies of Rad; apparently, he hadn't been nicknamed Bad Rad for his sunny disposition. Mike regaled me with tales of training camps past: when Bad Rad pushed his linemen through individual period, where they did drills over and over until muscle memory took over, exhaustion set in, or guys simply passed out. Bad Rad wasn't shy about his contributions to the game either. He loved to point out all the drills he had originated. When it was pointed out that a certain drill in which they were engaged had been made popular by another coach, Bad Rad came back with, "He plagiarized my mind."

And then, as legend has it, when all units came back together for team period, things went from bad to worse. If you weren't currently in the huddle and running plays, Bad Rad would have you working individual drills with other dying-to-rest offensive linemen. Standing around and sucking air was more than frowned upon; it wasn't permitted. If you weren't getting a gulp of water, you were working.

Webbie remembered lying down on the steps outside the locker room after one practice, sweating miserably from dehydration and the oppressive heat, too exhausted to walk over to the dining hall. He relayed the zombie-like trudge from the locker room to the non-air-conditioned Bonaventure Hall dorms, and sitting in the meeting rooms at night wishing for the simple grace of sleep to provide refuge from the ravages of Bad Rad.

According to Webbie, Rollie Dotsch—as tough and demanding a coach as I'd ever run across—was easy peasy compared to Bad Rad. I shuddered trying to comprehend something worse than what I was facing in that camp. Tunch, fellow rookie lineman Tyrone McGriff, and I were Rollie's personal whipping boys. The thought that there was someone tougher, more demanding, more intense than Rollie? *Yeesh.*

That someone, apparently, was named Bad Rad. He helped pioneer the art of "punching" after pass-protection rules changed. The change allowed offensive linemen to use their hands to keep a defensive lineman from grabbing them. Rad helped the cause by getting his linemen to wear tapered jerseys, using two-way tape on the shoulder pads to keep the defensive players from grabbing fistfuls of jersey in order to push-pull and ragdoll you. Though I came later, I was grateful to Bad Rad for his contributions. You can't know the frustration or helplessness of having a Joe Greene, L. C. Greenwood, Steve Furness, or Dwight White get "gription" on your jersey and throw you down on the ground, then face a honked-off Rollie as you sheepishly made your way back to the huddle. Or the frustration of getting pulled so hard

My mission was to protect the franchise at all costs. The franchise, in this case, was Terry Bradshaw (12). Courtesy of the Pittsburgh Steelers

that, on a stunt, you couldn't pass your man off or pick up the trailer on the twist.

Hear me now and believe me later, there's not too much worse on the football field than having to face Terry Bradshaw in the huddle after giving up a sack—or face Rollie Dotsch when you came back to the sideline.

I could tell you story upon story regarding the legacy of Bad Rad. From Gerry "Moon" Mullins leaning on the blocking sled in sheer exhaustion, saying, "Send me down the river, Rad" ("Trade me," in Mullins-speak) to Webbie telling Rad that he wouldn't go back out and play tackle in the second half against the Rams DE Jack Youngblood unless Rad went on TV and explained how Webbie had never played a snap at offensive tackle in his entire life. (Mike was beaten by Youngblood for two sacks in the second quarter when a lack of bodies forced him to play tackle.)

Despite the gory details, Radakovich was an innovator. Yes, he was intense. Yes, he could be harsh. And, yes, he certainly was demanding. But he was all about coaching and making you better. Bad Rad, it turns out, was the consummate teacher, one who was capable of coaching multiple positions. And one who helped and encouraged many, many others in his chosen profession. He was a throwback—a man who harkened back to the "tough love" coaching days, and one who was highly respected by his players and his peers. Countless coaches in high school, college, and pro ball owe their development and knowledge of the game to this tough guy from Duquesne, Pennsylvania, because he moved the game of football forward.

Bad Rad he was.

CHAPTER 13

SOMEBODY STOP HIM!

In the last chapter of my football life, in my role as radio broadcast analyst, and especially early on as a sideline reporter, the first thing I would do upon getting to the field was seek out the microphone stands on the sideline. Sometimes you have to be ready to be fully immersed in sound. Like the Monday night game the Steelers played against the Colts in 2005.

The noise level in that game at the Indianapolis RCA Dome was nightmarish. I thought I would go deaf, such was the din in that place. I had never experienced a louder stadium—and, folks, that's saying something. I literally had my headset turned all the way up just so I could hear Tunch and Billy Hillgrove upstairs during the broadcast. Rumors were rampant that the Colts pumped noise into the dome. From what I could see, there were mic stands placed some 10 to 20 yards apart and roughly 8 to 10 feet high, all with something that appeared to be a microphone positioned at the top. That's a lot of microphones returning an awful lot of decibels.

We returned for a second game that season—a playoff game—and I quickly noticed there were no microphone stands anywhere along the sidelines. They were gone. Coincidentally, the noise level for this game didn't quite reach the same frenetic level of noise as the first. Still, this was playoff football; frankly, a jet taking off in the RCA Dome wouldn't have drawn much notice. Though not artificially amped up this time, the crowd still roared in wavelike continuity. The hair on the back of my neck stood straight. There was electricity in the stadium, people, and the smell of pain was in the air.

Just after the coin toss, as the crescendo in the RCA Dome was building to another roar, the offensive unit of the Steelers grouped on the sideline near the end of the bench area in preparation to take the field. I took my place, standing a few yards (and more than a decade and a half removed) from being a part of that mass of players intermittently headbutting each other like mountain goats. Watching them, I could feel epic jolts of collisions past vibrating in my bones. How I wished to be among them just one more time! (Baby, once you've had that feeling, you never forget.)

Amid that high-octane, combustible, war-whooping offensive brotherhood, walked Ben Roethlisberger. He strode casually and calmly like a guy taking a stroll in South Park. Big Ben cruised down the sideline and stopped in front of me. He paused, then looked up into the swelling mass of humanity in the stands, seemingly noticing the near-hysterical masses for the first time. Slowly, a smile broke across his face and his eyes lit up like a kid's at Christmas. He began clapping his hands to the rhythm of the mayhem swirling about him, and then he broke out an even bigger smile, as if all the roaring in the building was intended just for him. Then, after delighting in the near-riotous atmosphere of the RCA Dome for a moment, he stopped to chat with one of the guys on the chain gang, the first-down-marker dude. I kid you not. I did a double take. He was joking with the guy! Moments from taking the field, with clashing helmets, testosterone, and sweat flying about him, Ben was nodding his head and smiling like a butcher's dog. He was telling a joke to an elder, "seasoned" citizen just prior to the biggest game of his young life. And it must have been a good joke too, because Ben seemed to enjoy the laugh as much as the guy on the chain gang did. Meanwhile, I was so nerved up I wanted to headbutt somebody while this young buck was calm and cool and telling jokes. I remember wondering, *Doesn't this guy understand what's at stake here?*

Apparently staying loose helped, because 10 plays and 5½ minutes later, Roethlisberger returned to the same—and now much quieter—Steelers bench area. He had completed six of seven passes, one for a touchdown to Antwaan Randle El. Ben didn't appear to be any more keyed up than when he'd gone on the field. If I thought beforehand that Ben didn't understand the enormity of the moment, I certainly understood once he came back to the bench that he had it all under control.

He was large and in charge, exuding a coolness that was calibrated somewhere between Terry Bradshaw and Clint Eastwood. Indeed, Ben remained that large and completely in charge throughout the game. His second TD pass to Heath Miller put the Steelers ahead 14–0, and the score hit 21–10 before the Colts rallied to get to 21–18. But by that point, Ben was tying the bow on a trip to Denver for the AFC Championship Game. With 1:20 remaining, the Steelers sacked Payton Manning on fourth down. Bill Cowher took off his headset and gave the proverbial power fist pump. Everyone knew that the game was all but over.

The Steelers took possession on the Indy 2, and everybody knew the ball was going to Jerome Bettis for the finishing score. The jumbo package was sent in, and the great Hines Ward flashed his megawatt smile on the sideline. The game was in the bag. Tunch, up in the booth, started talking about travel plans to Denver. Billy and I chided Tunch for being too cocky, too ready to say the game was over. "Don't jinx them," I was pleading. "Let the Bus put the nail in the coffin, and *then* we can talk about making travel plans."

And then it happened. The inconceivable, impossible, totally out-of-the-question, that-could-never-happen thing happened. The Bus fumbled.

One moment, I'm watching James Farrior and a couple of other players behind the Steelers bench area high-fiving the fans. Potsie actually gave away his gloves to one of them. The sudden roar from the Indianapolis fans jerked my attention back to the field, where I saw the pigskin pop into the air and tumble to the ground. Colts defensive back Nick Harper scooped it up and began sprinting the other way. I watched in horror as the plodding Steelers goal-line offense gave chase. I could not believe what my eyes were telling me. Over my headset I heard Tunch yell, "Somebody stop him!"

Roethlisberger suddenly found himself playing free safety. He backtracked, shifted his hips, dove, and made the play of the game by catching just enough of Harper's foot to bring him down. Farrior, hearing the roar and quickly assessing what had happened, sprinted past me. (I'm assuming to grab his gloves back.) He caught up to defensive coordinator Dick LeBeau, along with the rest of the defensive unit. The predominantly pro-Indy crowd that had quietly resigned themselves to the Steelers' looming victory suddenly roared like never before.

Manning began leading the Colts to a potential and wildly improbable come-from-behind victory. At the very least, a field goal would send the game into overtime. But the Colts' drive ground to a halt inside the Steelers' 30-yard line. A brilliant play by rookie CB Bryant McFadden, mano a mano with wide receiver Reggie Wayne, kept the Colts out of the end zone. Now fourth-and-2 at the Pittsburgh 28, the Steelers up 21–18 with 21 seconds showing on the clock, there was nothing but pain flashing across Bettis's face as he stood helpless on the sideline. The storybook ending of the Bus finishing his career with a Steelers Super Bowl appearance in his hometown of Detroit was suddenly in peril.

Colts kicker Mike Vanderjagt was at the time the most accurate kicker in NFL history. He stood 46 yards away from a tie and overtime. With tensions mounting to sky-high proportions just prior to the field goal attempt, Cowher called the obligatory timeout to freeze Vanderjagt. And then the kicker did the same thing we had just finished chiding Tunch for doing: he spoke too soon. During the timeout, Vanderjagt, obviously full confidence—and himself—turned toward the Steelers sideline and made an overconfident, mocking gesture.

With enough tension to blow the lid off the RCA Dome, both teams lined up for the kick. And it went right. Way right. Unutterably, unbelievably, inconceivably *way* wide right. So wide right it probably landed somewhere in Ohio. Almost as if he couldn't process what he had seen, Bettis's expression went from stone-cold misery to disbelief to a gradual understanding that the ending of his story wouldn't happen in Indianapolis.

Okay, Tunch, let's make those travel plans for Denver now!

CHAPTER 14

MAN ON THE MOON

Aside from all of the free food, one of the great things about broadcasting is the opportunity to cross paths with a wide spectrum of folks. That was especially true for me, working for the Pittsburgh Steelers. I've met people from different parts of the country, different vocations, even from different worlds.

Pregame always draws a pretty good smattering of fans with the good fortune of having secured a field pass to watch the Steelers warm up. Sometimes the players, if they're in a slightly playful mood, will interact with some of the spectators. My game-day duties as sideline analyst include a pregame hit from the radio booth high atop Heinz Field before heading to the field about an hour before kickoff. When I get to field level, it's always fun to catch up with everyone getting their own game-day duties done. There are also often celebrities hanging out, enjoying the buildup to kickoff. Former players love to come by, as well as musicians, actors, and athletes from other sports. And then every once in a while, you have a chance to meet someone who really blows your mind. That's where the man on the moon comes in.

Man on the Moon (1999) was a movie about the late, eccentric comedian Andy Kaufman, as played by Jim Carrey. The rock band R.E.M. wrote the 1992 song of the same name about Kaufman, and provided the soundtrack for the film. No, I didn't get to meet Andy Kaufman (who passed away in 1984), nor did I have the pleasure of meeting Jim Carrey; the man on the moon I got to meet was none other than the real deal: Buzz Aldrin.

A true American hero, Buzz was not only an engineer and command pilot in the United States Air Force, he was the lunar module pilot of the Apollo 11 mission. On July 20, 1969, he landed on the moon. He was the second human to set foot on that big piece of cheese in the sky. Nineteen minutes after mission commander Neil Armstrong touched the surface, Aldrin firmly planted his feet on the moon as well, looked around, and said, "Beautiful view." Then, responding to Armstrong's "Isn't it magnificent?" Buzz uttered, "Magnificent desolation."

I've always been a fan of NASA and space exploration. Hey, I grew up watching the Robinson family on *Lost in Space*. Then there was *Star Trek* and Spock, *Star Wars* and Yoda.... I even took the time to master Spock's "Live long and prosper" hand gesture. As a kid growing up, I thrilled to the televised sights and sounds of rockets blasting up from the launch pads at Cape Kennedy. I lived through the space race between the United States and Russia. And though I was just 11 years old when Aldrin and Armstrong touched down on the moon, I do remember sitting around the TV. There we were—my mom and dad; older sister, Linrae; younger sister, Joy; and still younger brother Ron—watching in black and white as the most famous line in human history, "One small step for man, one giant leap for mankind," came over the airwaves. It was truly magnificent.

So I was out there shooting the breeze on the sideline when I got wind that Buzz Aldrin was there, and would I like to meet him? *Are you kidding me?* Proper introductions were made, and I can sincerely say that of all the big shooters who've graced the Steelers sideline—from Charlie Daniels and Hank Williams Jr. to Russell Crowe, Arnie Palmer, and even Rush Limbaugh—shaking the hand of Buzz Aldrin was my greatest thrill. It was difficult to come to grips, literally and figuratively, with the thought that I was shaking the hand of history and courage such as I had never experienced. Comprehending what he had accomplished in his lifetime was mind-blowing.

I use "come to grips" figuratively, because this man represented a profile in courage such as the world has rarely seen, or will again. A graduate of West Point, like my oldest son, Kyle, Buzz was a fighter pilot in the Korean War and flew 66 combat missions downing enemy fighter jets. He was a pilot on the Gemini 12 space mission. He set a record, spending five hours outside the space capsule, demonstrating that astronauts could work safely outside the spacecraft. The list of his accomplishments is bigger than this book. He is truly an American legend. I mean,

You never know who you'll run into while working as a sideline reporter for the Pittsburgh Steelers. This day, it was Franco Harris. Courtesy of the Pittsburgh Steelers

the man is Wyatt Earp, Jim Bowie, Daniel Boone, with a dose of Paul Bunyan all wrapped into one.

I say "come to grips" literally too, because he had a handshake of steel. I have a fairly decent grip myself, but this guy's was solid. At that point Buzz was in his eighties, but he had the grip of a man half his age and twice as big. He had piercing eyes that took you in and sized you up. He seemed like the type who didn't need much time to decide whether he liked or disliked you. I felt at ease with him immediately.

As you might imagine, I was pretty much beside myself. I mean, I tried to act cool, but frankly when you meet the King of Cool—the second man ever to walk on the moon, the first guy to take a leak on the moon, the first guy to have communion on the moon—well, I'll admit I lost my cool. We started off talking about the Steelers and the day's opponent. Then we started to talk about him and his long career. The conversation moved to the moon, and I was angling for one of my favorite conspiracy stories—a supposed sighting of a UFO on the moon, a comment allegedly made, then retracted, by Aldrin on the Apollo 11 mission. So I brought up the Apollo 11 mission, but he quickly broke off to tell me about his high school football days. I'm listening patiently, but gadzooks, man, you went to the freaking moon! Forget football! Still, he even made the tales of his football days sound exciting and fun.

Yet all the while, the countdown clock in my head was ticking, reminding me that I soon had to do a sideline hit. I was running out of time. Unfortunately, I had work to do. Artfully (or so I thought), I craftily attempted to get the conversation back to the moon mission. I mean, I *had* to find out if there were aliens lurking about while Neil and Buzz were out cruising in their moon mobile! But just then, Buzz, as boisterous as I am, threw his arms up and had a sudden flashback. It was a memory about a high school championship. I could see the sparkle in his eyes as he told the story.

My mental clock continued to tick its way to the witching hour, and then it came, that inevitable moment when I had to excuse myself and hurry away to do my shtick. I was running late, because I wanted to milk every moment with Buzz that I could. Let me tell you, it was only with great—and I do mean this in all sincerity, *great*—reluctance, followed by another round of clasping hands and another moment of marveling at his strength, that I moved on to my duties.

I don't know that I've ever regretted departing from a conversation more. But I do know without a shadow of a doubt that conversing and shaking hands with Buzz Aldrin was not only a high-water mark in my life but a moment in time that I will never forget and forever cherish. Legitimate American heroes are few and far between. Rare is the man of extraordinary courage and skill whose very life reads like an adventure novel, and yet Buzz Aldrin is all that and more. The man on the moon.

CHAPTER 15

DUTY, HONOR, AND COUNTRY

The start of the 2016 NFL schedule found the Steelers on the road in the nation's capital, the Washington Redskins hosting Pittsburgh in the first *Monday Night Football* broadcast of the season.

During pregame warm-ups, after checking out what was happening on the field and sussing out any developing storylines, I did my celeb flyby to see which luminaries had shown up. As I'm sitting, there came Maury Povich. Then I saw actor Matthew McConaughey. And then the NFL commish, Roger Goodell, walked toward me on the sideline. What better than to ambush him into an unscheduled interview, live and without a net?

Goodell was agreeable. And no, despite being a Jamestown, New York, native, he still hadn't been to the Lucille Ball Film Festival held there every year. (Ball was a Jamestown native herself.) Tsk-tsk. Being a western New York guy myself, you know I had to ask.

I had some microphone trouble after I did my pregame hit, so just before kickoff I had to run back upstairs to the radio booth, where our on-site engineer for the Steelers Radio Network, Greg Resh, was working. I had to hustle because they had already flipped the coin. So as I rolled around the corner and back into the elevator, my mind was working on elements of the game that I wanted to feature once I got back down. But when I hit the elevator, I stopped dead in my tracks. There, in the corner, wearing a baseball cap pulled low over his eyes and looking about as threatening as a librarian, was a man I knew by sight instantly. He was someone whom you might glance at, and then dismiss, without so much as a second thought. Unless, of course, you knew who he was. And me? I knew immediately that it was Robert O'Neill, the man who killed Osama bin Laden.

I have to say once again that over the course of my playing and broadcasting careers, I've been blessed and privileged to have met a number of amazing men and women. Yet O'Neill stands alone. I honestly think my jaw would have hit the ground if it were long enough.

There were several people accompanying him in the elevator, and they formed a semi-protective half-circle around him. Add in some Redskins staff personnel who were ushering him to and from the field, where he oversaw the coin toss, and we had nearly a full elevator. He leaned into the corner of the elevator, buried in his phone and with people surrounding him. I simply couldn't help but be a tad overwhelmed thinking of the tremendous service this man had rendered to his country—not to mention the small semblance of some type of closure for the many, many families who had been victimized, traumatized, and had their lives ripped apart by 9/11.

For a brief second, as some late add-ons crammed into the already full elevator, people jostled for position as the elevator started its long, slow climb to the top of the stadium. As we ascended, I was transported back in time. Years flew by in a nanosecond. Suddenly it was 2006. My wife, Faith, and I were at West Point with our oldest son, Kyle, for freshman orientation. He was about to begin his first day as a West Point cadet. We had dutifully filed, per instructions, into Eisenhower Hall at 6:00 AM. After a 20-minute welcome speech delivered to an auditorium of nervous parents and cadets, the officer addressing the group suddenly stopped and said simply, "Cadets, you have 90 seconds to say your goodbyes."

I was stunned. I wasn't prepared for such an abrupt departure. Sure, I was certain Kyle knew what he was signing up for when he applied to West Point. But I'm not sure I had fully developed my sense of what it all meant in the big picture. Of course, West Point is an incredible academic institution with an incredible campus. The men and women who attend are some of the finest, most accomplished young people in the world: gifted, talented, resolute, and determined. But it was also a school that churned out military leaders. And where there are military leaders, there is also the possibility of military action (or, in another word, war). Maybe that's when it hit me. Kyle was leaving the comfy confines of life at home to undergo the rigors of basic training in the outback of West Point.

I had prepared a few words to share with my son, but as I stood up to shake his hand, reality immediately set in. An overwhelming sense came over me that this was too big for Kyle. That I was allowing him to—*what*? What was I allowing, or *not* allowing? Well, I realized that it wasn't about me anymore. He was a man now. It was his choice. And there it was in a nutshell. My son was now a man, fully capable of making his own decisions and making his way in the world. The full weight of it dropped on me, as crushing as the time I dropped a York 45-pound weight plate on my foot. Sudden. And the clear pain focused me in the moment.

Tears flooded my eyes. I choked up, unable to speak. Looking into Kyle's eyes, I began to feel the very first pangs of what real sacrifice, real blood treasure, looked like and felt like, as it was being offered up to military service. I have often heard people talk about how hard deployments are on the families of our armed forces. And sure, I had seen camouflage-uniformed men and women disembarking at airports over the years. Hugs between husband and wife, parent and child, pregnant, newlyweds, all carrying almost a palpable sense of honor, intensity, and desperation in the last milliseconds of those embraces. I observed them respectfully from a distance but never personally experienced that last hug. I could never quite relate. Until now.

Now, post-9/11. Now, the hunt for bin Laden. Now, the Iraq War. Now, Saddam Hussein being hunted. And now, our oldest son stood on the precipice of taking his place in the heralded Long Gray Line of West Point. *Are you kidding me? Ninety seconds?* I mean, I thought we might tag along through part of the day. Maybe watch and cheer? I don't know.

I should've listened to Faith, who'd served in the air force. She tried warning me that there was no room for warm fuzziness in military school. Boy, she was right. And there I was, a dad who couldn't even crack a joke. *Nothing.* I stood there stupidly, desperately searching to restrain my emotions. Where were the practiced few words I had chosen that would bolster my son with wisdom? *C'mon man! At least give him some of that time-tested "Go get 'em, son!" bravado.* Nope. I failed miserably.

It was my Kyle who, thankfully, manned up and saved the moment. He looked me square in the eyes, hugged me, firmly shook my hand, smiled, and said, "I know, Dad." And then he was gone. Kyle would never be the same. And neither would I.

I found myself stirred back to the present day by the quiet hum of the elevator, realizing that I was staring dumbly at O'Neill. I moved through the semicircle and stood nearby as a few more people packed into the elevator at the next stop. Though I was much bigger than him, I felt so small standing next to him. I knew I wanted to thank him for the justice he had helped to mete out, for his sacrifices over the years in the rigors of training, for the dangers endured in the more than 400 combat missions he had faced, for the fearful times in which his family had languished while he was deployed on those missions.

My mind time-traveled yet again, to April 2010, back to Fort Benning, Georgia. Kyle had just completed 11 weeks of brutal Ranger School training. Faith and I had driven down to watch Kyle graduate with his class. General David Petraeus, whose son was in Kyle's Ranger class, would be giving the graduation address. We were driving on base to pick up Kyle. Apparently, the training was so rigorous that the soldiers aren't allowed to do anything physical, even drive a vehicle. Having been through a number of really tough training camps and football games, I thought they were acting a little overprotective. I couldn't have been more wrong. (And over the course of my life, I've gotten pretty good at being wrong.)

We drove past two men who were sitting on a bench alongside the road. Faith said, "Look, there's Kyle!"

I laughed and said, "That's not Kyle!" and drove by. I didn't even recognize my own son.

With my son Kyle at a recent Steelers game.

Faith adamantly insisted it was him. We slowed down, turned around, and pulled over. Sure enough, she was right. The young man who slowly rose to his feet from the bench barely resembled my son. The strapping, muscled-up, tough-as-leather 172-pounder of a Ranger School hopeful of 11 weeks ago was now somewhere around 140 pounds. I mean, I weighed 140 in third grade! Needless to say, I was shocked. Hugging my son, I noticed then how drained, depleted, and tired he was. He moved as slowly as I did on Monday mornings after a Sunday game. It was eye-opening. I was used to hardship, I was used to physical pain, but it always was in the context of a game. There were referees and rules; there were penalty flags and time clocks. What my son had just survived was one thing. But what he was preparing to do next was opening up a kaleidoscope of multihued worries and anxieties. This was no game. This was preparation for future deployment, for combat.

We most humbly and proudly watched a few days later as Kyle stood with the other Ranger School graduates while General Petraeus addressed them. By this time I had grown accustomed to the emaciated, starving looks of Kyle and his fellow classmates. During the speech, a Ranger School graduate in the front row passed out while standing at ease—I kid you not. The young man suddenly wobbled and then face-planted.

The rest of the group responded like an Indy 500 pit crew. They separated right down the middle of the company, dragged the unconscious soldier to the rear of the formation, and everyone filled in for him so quickly that I had to rub my eyes and make sure I had seen what I thought I had. It literally couldn't have taken more than 20 seconds from start to finish. It still makes me shake my head that the depths of suffering and forced deprivation of food and sleep could cause a man to lose all strength and vitality. Nearly a week after finishing Ranger School, while just standing and listening to a man speak, you go dark on your feet and lose consciousness. Man, that's being tapped out.

Back to reality again. With the memory of that poor, young soldier fading into the recesses of my mind, I looked again at O'Neill. I didn't want to bother him, but I knew I had to speak. To thank him on behalf of all the families so affected by the 9/11 attack. To thank him on behalf of all the families of the military community of sons and daughters who have also sacrificed time, memories, body parts, and even lives in doing their part defending our freedoms.

The elevator slowed as we approached another floor. The grinding hum momentarily receded and I floated back to July 2011. I was sitting on a screened-in porch in a little place we called our weekend home in Harrisville, Ohio. I was looking at my warrior/son, who was leaving home the next day to deploy for a year to Afghanistan. I was brimming with love for this man so full of life, so strong, so young. My heart was in my stomach. *He's going off to war. Not to a game. Not a weekend trip to the coast. He's being deployed to a hostile region on the backside of the earth somewhere. And I am afraid.* We'd just finished discussing a letter he wrote to me that was being held by the United States Army, based upon the presupposition that should he not return from Afghanistan, I was to receive this letter. There is no more searing, sobering moment between a father and a son than that, period. It burns in my memory like acid and scars me to this day.

Over the intervening years, I have come to a greater understanding and appreciation of the cost of freedom. What the Long Gray Line is really all about. That duty, honor, and country are more than just words to be recited mindlessly. And that those who adhere to those words are more than just people you unpack and throw out there on the battlefield at a time of war. They are family treasures. They are sons and daughters. They are brothers and sisters. They are husbands and wives. They are loved.

All my life I have thought of myself as a tough guy, someone who has overcome a great many obstacles and challenges, faced adversity, and still stood tall. Now had come the dim realization that I was foolish, and fooling myself. I was nothing. I had accomplished nothing. I mean, I played a game! As I hugged Kyle one last time with a sense of intensity, desperation, and longing just like I had seen from others in airports over the years, I realized that my son was everything I had ever hoped to be yet had fallen so far short of becoming. I learned at that moment that there was a higher honor than playing in the NFL. Standing before me—looking every bit the warrior I had sought to become in my football career—was the part of me that lived "duty, honor, and country" in a way I never could. Here was a man who would go on to withstand the rigors of real war, not the metaphorical NFL battle his father fought. Here was a man who would go on to endure trials and conflicts, improvised explosive devices, and combat, and take his place among the hallowed hall of the true brotherhood of heroes and warriors. My son. A true warrior. A true American hero. *My* hero.

Words stopped. Acknowledgment of the inevitable dropped in on us, and there came that final moment of desperate intensity. I didn't want to let him go. "You, you come back to me, you hear?" was all I barely croaked as Kyle turned and walked away. He was walking the true path of the warrior: square shoulders, purposeful steps, a totally different man than the boy who had entered West Point just a few years before. A warfighter. Some are called, few are chosen. Even fewer are called to step forward into actual battle. It takes a special man to become a warfighter. Don't fool yourself into thinking you're as tough as them. You aren't. Neither am I.

The elevator bumped to a stop, jostling me from that hard-to-revisit moment. But in that quick interlude I had made up my mind. Just before the doors opened, I stepped forward to Mr. O'Neill, extended my hand, and simply said, "Thank you." I didn't introduce myself. I didn't try to engage in conversation. I did the only thing that a father of a fellow fighting man could do in a situation such as this: be appreciative of the courage, dedication, and valor of those who stand guard over the very freedoms we take for granted so easily.

O'Neill looked up at me, surprise briefly crossing his eyes. I'm fairly certain this had happened many times to him. His handshake was firm, his eyes locked with mine in quick assessment.

"I have a son who serves," I said.

"Thank him for his service for me," he said in return. And with that I stepped out of the elevator, from the time machine that had transported me through portals of memory. The door closed, and Robert O'Neill, the man who killed Osama bin Laden, was gone.

My last, fleeting thought as I stepped into the radio booth to get my gear fixed was hugging then–Captain Kyle Jacob Wolfley of the United States Army at the Pittsburgh Airport in the summer of 2012. After guiding him through a year of deployment in Afghanistan, helping him survive multiple IEDs and combat, God had brought him home healthy and in one piece. And a smile crossed my face.

I still remember Kyle's reaction to my much-too-long and overwhelming bear hug. "Dad, uh, Dad, it's okay. You're good. You can let go now." Hugs have never been so sweet.

CHAPTER 16

IT'S ALWAYS BEEN A CIRCUS

What has been will be again,
what has been done will be done again;
there is nothing new under the sun.
—Ecclesiastes 1:9

By most reactions, there is a growing unrest in Steelers Country. Behavior detrimental to the ballclub, team goals, or other teammates isn't a recent development. It's happened before, and it'll happen again.

Sure, I get the fan reaction. I'm not here defending bad deeds or conduct unbecoming. But to say that what's been going on is a circus, the insinuation that all discipline has broken down, is ridiculous—and simply not fair. What the average fan is watching is real life, real people living out real lives, and real people displaying both good and bad characteristics of the human condition. (And you thought *stra-tee-gery* and clock management were the hardest parts of being a head coach.)

The real challenge for the head coach is managing those very same people who create the issues—to get the best out of them and develop a chemistry that has everyone rowing in the same direction. It's always been that way. So much happens behind closed doors, folks. In the sanctity of the locker room, away from the public's eye, most people assume everything is copacetic within those four walls because their newsfeed isn't flashing an update on their iPhone. Then suddenly we're all confronted with a tweet, headline, or soundbite from Lev Bell, Antonio Brown, George Pickens, or someone else. All I'm saying is that with today's modern technology, it could have just easily been Joe Greene, Ernie Holmes, Tunch Ilkin, or me. Name the decade; there were antics.

Depending on whether you're winning or losing, the interpretations of what's going on inside those four walls begin to dominate the news cycle, and in turn, people's opinions. Obviously, certain disciplinary actions need to be taken, and they will be. But folks, this is nothing new. It's been that way since the time of Chuck Noll, on through Bill Cowher, and now into the Mike Tomlin era. You simply cannot house 53 healthy alpha males loaded with testosterone in one room and expect everyone to function like the Brady Bunch. No—you'll have guys acting out, guys losing their way, guys not acting like the guys they once were. It happens. The key, really, is that most people didn't know about it because the media landscape has changed so much.

Antonio Brown showed up at training camp in a helicopter. But hey, at least he didn't shoot at it, the way Ernie Holmes did back in the day. (See chapter 30 for more on that story.) I remember Steve Courson nearly shooting Steelers nose tackle Gary Dunn on an off-day during the season. We used to call the Tuesdays after film review "shoots-in-fest" days. Everybody used to bring their guns, weaponry of all sorts, and we'd go to a gun range. Ted Peterson even had a scale-model Civil War cannon. Anyway, we'd hop on to our two- and three- and four-wheelers and go shoot guns. It was a great way to let off steam with the boys. Until Gary dove off his four-wheeler when bullets accidentally whizzed past him. Now, imagine if the press had gotten hold of *that*.

And speaking of *The Brady Bunch*, I don't believe Noll, Cowher, or Tomlin ever coached anyone like Aaron Hernandez. Just saying.

No, Antonio should never have streamed Mike T's postgame speech live from the locker room. It was bad judgment on A.B.'s part in a moment of elation. But I don't for a moment think he did that maliciously. It was one of those new things that evolved from technology that hadn't been encountered yet. It was. And it hasn't happened since.

But think about it. Wasn't it back in 2014 when Ravens coach John Harbaugh's postgame speech aired on CBS? That had some colorful language in it, including a swipe at the Steelers. As I recall, Harbaugh was none too happy about it. And speaking of the Ravens, didn't Ray Lewis have a few bad behavior issues during his career?

We used to have a sign that hung on all four walls of the Three Rivers Stadium locker room. It read, *What you see here, what you do here, what you say here, stays here when you leave here.* I'm a big believer in keeping family business in-house. And let me tell you, that sign was adhered to by all players back in my day. And even then, an overenthusiastic fan once overheard a player having dinner at a restaurant. The player aired a few grievances and bellyached about some things in a private conversation to his wife. Well, that fan called one of the talk shows to repeat what he had just overheard. It was then broadcast and rebroadcast for a week throughout the city. You betcha that created a dust-up. But the guys worked it out; they took care of it in-house.

Hey, I know better than most not to cast stones. As a young player with more testosterone than brains, I had a Kellen Winslow Jr. moment. I stood before a camera postgame and idiotically compared it to war. Moments later, *off*-camera, away from any microphones, I was taken to task by Rocky Bleier and set straight. I don't believe that I made that same mistake again. And to this day, I am grateful for the Rock's intervention. Thankfully, the 24/7 news cycle was in its infancy back in the 1980s. The power of the social media phenomenon had yet to be discovered.

Joey Porter once went after Ray Lewis after a game and challenged him to a fight. Tunch and I had Coach's back at midfield when Chuck Noll did the same to Oilers head coach Jerry Glanville after a bitter, hard-fought game in Houston. Antonio Brown had an anger issue and threw a temper tantrum during a Chiefs game. Okay, not one of his better moments, I'll grant you.

I've had my fair share, to be sure. I was once reprimanded but good for a little helmet-throwing, kicking-stuff, hissy-fit meltdown on the sideline during a game. Another time I became enraged at one of my coaches and challenged *him* to a fight. Nobody heard about that; it stayed in-house. And then there was me, yet again, angrily in the face of a reporter, only to have him explain he wasn't the person I thought he was.

I stupidly mixed him up with another writer with whom I had a beef. It was all absolutely inexcusable, stupid, moronic stuff, that now, in my older years, it makes me cringe.

I remember a very, *very* angry Mike Webster grabbing an assistant coach by the collar of his shirt and reading him the riot act during a practice. And physically throwing a 300-pound-plus nose tackle at Chuck Noll because he was honked off at Coach. But they (and we) worked it out—in private, away from cameras, microphones, and all things media-driven.

When Tony Dungy had to intervene in the hallway of Three Rivers Stadium and pull two assistant coaches off each other, thank goodness it was halftime and there were no TV cameras around. They worked it out.

And when Joe Greene and Jack Lambert nearly got into a fistfight and had to be pulled apart on the sideline during a game against Cleveland, Coach Noll saw what was happening and headed the other way. Joe and Jack? After the game they went into the equipment room and worked it out.

Shoot, I remember Tunch Ilkin once punched Noll when Coach tried to intervene and caught a little misguided friendly fire during a practice flare-up between teammates. Mel Blount sued Noll for defamation. Chuck fined Mean Joe for kicking in a door. Ask Jason Gildon and some of the other Cowher-era players about the free-for-all in the locker room when teammates took up heavy wooden stools, brandishing them as weapons. How's all of that for divisiveness and communication breakdown?

That doesn't excuse any bad behavior nowadays, but it also doesn't mean chaos has taken over and the apocalypse is upon us. Barnum and Bailey and the Ringling Brothers have not checked in to town. Look, there was no absence of discipline in any of the three eras. Coach Noll didn't "lose" the locker room; Tunch didn't get cut from the errant infraction. Players didn't stop playing for Cowher. Mel and Chuck worked it out. In fact, the great leader of our great dynasty, Joe Greene, credits Chuck's tutelage to this day for helping him grow as a man.

Football is a high-velocity, high-tension, testosterone-fueled pursuit that isn't for everybody. Lapses in judgment will and do occur. Egregious errors are known to happen. Yet if cooler heads prevail, things can usually be worked out one way or another. It may require player movement, but that's not for us to say. The in-house community knows better than any of us sitting on the outside.

These things happen all the time—not just in Pittsburgh but in other cities and on other teams. I can tell you stories of the Buffalo Bills and Jim Haslett and Fred Smerlas nearly coming to blows with each other in the huddle during a game. I could tell you about the great former Steelers defensive lineman and Dallas assistant coach Ernie Stautner giving a vein-popping, purple facemelt to one of his players on the sideline while I happened that way.

The late, great Raider John Matuszak was once kicked out of a meeting while carrying a boom box on his shoulder. Ted Hendricks "protested" Tom Flores over a lack of playing time with a glass of wine while seated at an umbrella-covered table near the practice field. I could tell you about guys late to meetings (including me), guys walking out of meetings (Ernie Holmes), guys getting traded during meetings (Steve Courson), guys missing meetings (Rod Woodson)—you name it.

The difference in all of this is whether or not the fans hear about it. With news cycles being what they are, and social media adding to the cannonade of blaring headlines, chances are you're going to hear about poor conduct in this day and age. Back in the day, not so much. When I hear people say Chuck wouldn't have put up with it, I say reread this chapter. And let's be perfectly clear: that is not a shot at Coach Noll. I loved the man. He changed the trajectory of my life. I'm forever grateful for his leadership and mentorship. He's indisputably one of the greatest influencers in my life.

Misguided individuals will try to tell me Bill Cowher would have had none of it. Honestly, folks, you're simply kidding yourselves if you believe that. Cowher was a great coach. And he had the reputation of being a heavy-handed disciplinarian. But I will tell you, he wasn't nearly as heavy-handed as people think. When James Harrison refused to acknowledge Cowher screaming at him to get his attention from the sideline of a game in Buffalo, it wasn't because he couldn't hear Bill. No, Deebo was angry and defiant. He refused to acknowledge his coach. And did James suffer any repercussions? No. They took care of it in-house.

Mike Tomlin is a great coach as well. And he has 21st-century discipline issues he must handle. There are player infractions and issues that have to be dealt with and will be dealt with. Coaching back in the day was different. Those coaches could run you, they could beat on you until you quit, they could make life unbearable. There were no salary caps and free agency. When Coach Noll thought that he'd had it with being Mr. Nice Guy, it was time for a "purge." I lived through one in 1984. It was brutal, simply the hardest training camp I'd ever experienced. Usually players worry about being cut. The saying in camp that year became, "What's the worst thing they can do to you? They can keep you."

A tough training camp tends to shake things up. It creates a survivor mentality, a little humility, and some bloodshed. And that's okay. A little bloodletting is good. But if you think player discipline and having to deal with player issues are strictly Pittsburgh phenomena, you are sorely mistaken. And if you think that the discipline problems of today's player are exclusive to this modern era only, again you are misguided.

It's the way it's always been. Someone gets out of line, take care of it in-house. If that doesn't work, a change of scenery might be beneficial. And if that doesn't work, at some point, unemployment will take care of what the others couldn't.

We've seen it before; we'll see it again. There is nothing new under the sun.

CHAPTER 17
MOUTHGUARDS AND MAYHEM

Mouthguards are a necessary evil. I get that. I remember going to a sporting goods store with my mother when I was in seventh grade so I could play intramural football. We went into the store, bought the mouthguard, took it home, and I partially read the directions. Note the key word: *partially*. The part that I read involved the boiling of water, sticking the mouthguard into the pan of boiling water until it began to soften, and then sticking it into my mouth to mold around my teeth. Okay, so I missed the part about letting it cool before jamming it into my piehole. Let me tell you this: nothing says "reread the directions" like a mouthful of molten mouthguard. (I should probably explain at this point that partially read directions would become a recurring theme of mine in the years to come.)

Anyway, mouthguards were a necessary evil throughout my high school, college, and into my rookie pro year of football. If you've never had the pleasure of having a chunk of molded plastic stuck into your mouth and played football, man, you don't know what you're missing. Those mouthguards can get real funky when they're strapped onto helmets. I don't care how much of a clean freak you are, mouthguards get nasty after a while. Most guys might wash that thing every now and then, sure, but if the personal hygiene habits of their youth tended toward the sloppy side, brother, you might witness a biological experiment growing inside that thing. I *have* seen green mouthguards, yes.

The referees are sticky on that stuff too. They would throw flags if your mouthguard wasn't in your mouth. Coaches were always yelling to "Put your mouthguard in!" And of course my mother was always on me about wearing one. She and my dad apparently spent a small fortune on my teeth growing up, so I should show my appreciation by protecting them, said Mom. She would approach me like an Old West horse trader and push my mouth open to look inside and make sure I wasn't damaging my chompers. That woman was a force of nature.

What I really hated about the mouthguards, besides the nastiness they would inevitably develop, was how they hindered your breathing and gave you excessive dry mouth during warm-weather games. The inside of your cheek and gums might be raw and bloodied by the end of the game from the dadgum mouthguard rubbing against them.

I wore a mouthguard throughout my rookie year, and one of the funniest things that ever happened to me occurred during a preseason game. I was on a slide protection, meaning that after checking the inside linebacker, I would slide out to pick up a possible blitzing outside linebacker. As I kick-stepped out from my left guard position, I naturally exhaled forcefully through my mouth. In doing so, my mouthguard caught air and popped out, as if I had meant to spit it out. But the funnier part was my reaction. I didn't realize it at the time, but my first reflex was to try to catch it on the fly by slapping my hands together. Well, I missed, and continued on my path outside to pick up the blitzing linebacker.

Having lost the mouthguard, I finished the game without it. But the game film we watched two days later provided a real chuckle for my offensive line coach, Rollie Dotsch, who had never seen one of his guys spit out his mouthguard, try to catch it in the air without missing a beat, and then continue on with his assignment. He showed that film over and over. I guess it's always nice to be a first at something.

The next week we were in Dallas for a night game, which started at nine o'clock. Texas was in the middle of a heatwave, and the thermometer was still hovering above 90 degrees at kickoff. It was my first start at left guard, and I can't tell you how excited I was anticipating this game. The first start is special, it really is, and even though it was technically just a preseason game, it was still a start. And as the old saying goes, that opportunity to become a starter may only come around once, so be ready to go.

I also played special teams. Back in the day, starters on the offense or defense still played a lot of special teams, and I was on the kickoff return unit. I believe I was on the punt team as well. Anyway, I knew going in it was going to be a long, hot evening.

And it was one long, hot game, to be sure. It was *brutal.* That heat-wave that smothered Dallas made for a scorcher. During a timeout in the huddle, out on the field at Texas Stadium, my mouth was so dry it felt as if there were a bunch of cuts inside it. The feeling reminded me of a time when I had to go to the dentist's office as a kid. A kindly gent, the dentist shot my cheek up with Novocain before working on a cavity. I thought it pretty cool for a while afterward that I could bite the inside of my mouth and feel no pain...right up until the Novocain wore off. Well, that's what the inside of my mouth felt like now. And my mouthguard felt like it was melting into the roof of my mouth. I was miserable. I remember noticing that Tunch hadn't worn a mouthguard, and neither had Mike Webster.

Almost gagging on the stupid thing, I remember thinking, *Why do I bother?* With that final thought, I lifted my head up, gathered what little spit was available, and with one big *pfffwhttt!* spit out the accursed mouthguard, never to be worn again over the remaining 11 years of my career. I never gave another thought to it either. Sure, my mom kept harping on me when she noticed I wasn't wearing it, and every now

Did I wear my mouthguard when I boxed pro wrestler Butterbean in 2002? You bet I did!

Wolf List: My Top 10 Funniest Moments in the NFL

Life in the NFL could often be a grind, but you can't accuse us of never having any fun with it. Here are 10 of my favorite funny moments from on and off the field that still have us rollin'.

10. Beer Bash: Joking with Webby about drinking an unopened can of beer that had been thrown at us from the Dawg Pound.
9. Turkish Delight: The time Tunch almost got me to unwittingly say a very bad Turkish curse word when I met his mother the first time.
8. No Joy: When my sister took the call from Chuck Noll that would change my life.
7. No More: Finding an ingenious way to stop my fellow rookie and roommate Tunch from snoring.
6. Mic Drop: The time Steelers VP Tony Quatrini told me he might have to tackle Myron Cope for control of the microphone at halftime.
5. Flash Bang: Terrifying a nearby referee by telling him about my family's history with lightning.
4. *Not* OK: My one-on-one Oklahoma drill with "Mean" Joe Greene in Latrobe.
3. Rollin', Rollin', Rollin': Tricking Tunch into a rookie duet of "Rawhide" in training camp.
2. Friendly Fire: Spearing Tunch in the keister and not disclosing who did it until it was all revealed on film.
1. Incoming: Tunch projectile vomiting into the Cleveland Browns nose tackle's face.

and then she'd demand an inspection. But considering my newly formed mouthguard freedom, I wasn't going back to that tyranny anytime soon.

That is, until I started boxing. Over the years I had developed an interest in the martial arts and boxing. I trained intermittently in boxing, wu wei chuan lum, kali, wing chun, jujitsu, and other styles throughout my playing days, and when I retired I kicked my training into high gear. In the absence of football, I trained multiple times a day, sometimes upward of eight hours. It really sucks you in, trust me.

And then Faith and I opened a gym. We had a boxing team, and it was great fun. We often held open sparring sessions with guys from different gyms. We would round-robin in the ring, so you might go several rounds and then sit out several rounds. On one occasion, after sparring four or five rounds in a row, I sat out for four or five. So I jumped down from the ring, took my gloves and headgear off, and took my mouthguard out and placed it on top of a piece of clean plastic sitting on the edge of the ring. I watched and coached from the outside of the ring over the next half dozen rounds, slugging water and offering encouragement to everybody. I always viewed sparring as an opportunity to exchange information. I never thought of it as competition, because then egos got in the way and it tended to make everyone rely on their strengths instead of trying to upgrade their weaknesses.

Well, when it was my turn to get back in the ring, I put my headgear back on, grabbed my mouthguard, jammed it in, and then put my boxing gloves back on. I climbed through the ropes while chewing on my mouthguard, trying to get it to settle in over my teeth. *Hmmm. Something is wrong.* No matter how I turned the mouthguard over and over, bit into it, chewed on it some more, and then tried to lube it up with saliva, it just seemed like it wouldn't settle on my teeth. Like maybe it wasn't...

It wasn't my mouthguard!

Oh, sweet Marie! I spit out the offending item with prejudice, as they say, and began rubbing my tongue with my equally unsanitary boxing gloves. Smelling the sweat-drenched boxing gloves kickstarted my innards, and nausea began to roll over me in waves. You can guess the rest of the story, but to this day I don't know how my mouthguard got mixed up with somebody else's. Nobody admitted to owning the stupid thing, or moving mine, but I do know for sure that mouthguard wasn't mine.

Ugh.

CHAPTER 18

I HATE LIGHTNING

I was standing in the huddle during the two-minute warning at Riverfront Stadium in Cincinnati as the sky above us crackled with the electricity that only a lightning storm can bring with it. You might have thought it was fireworks night in the 'Burgh, such was the firepower erupting over our heads. This was back in the day when lightning didn't seem to be too high on anyone's list of potentially harmful conditions on a football field. But I *hate* lightning. Always have.

Some of my earliest childhood memories consist of my slightly wild-eyed father running around shepherding his kids into the house upon the first crack of a distant thunderstorm. My dad being scared was enough in itself to put the fear into me. When you're a little dude and Dad is yelling, "What are ya, crazy? Get in the house, for crying out loud! Don't you hear that lightning?" Goose bumps. Of course, my dad never really understood that it was thunder you heard and lightning you saw. But he did understand that it was lightning that killed.

So, yes, he passed that fear down to me, and thus the fear of lightning became generational. Years later, when my daughter Megan was 12 or 13 and playing with friends at the end of the street, thunder started to roll in from a distance, and my Mad Hatter–crazy, white-hot Wolfley fear of lightning kicked in. "Megan!" I shouted, sweating like I had just run all the way from the house to the park, which I had. I grabbed her like I was carrying a football and started to run back toward the house. It was at this point, with the thunder and distant lightning framing my thoughts, that I managed to come to my senses and recognize that her friends needed to come with us as well. Suffice it to say, Megan was mortified that her big, strong dad was panic-stricken. Yeah, it *was* kind of embarrassing. And I'm not even going to mention the slide episode with my oldest son, Kyle, when he was small. I'm pretty sure I scarred him for life too. Boy, I must say, those terrifying memories of thunder and lightning are deeply embedded within my psyche. Maybe even fused to my DNA.

Boom! Boom! Boom! And so it started in the game. Thunder, then lightning. First from a distance, and then like an advancing army suddenly closing in on Riverfront Stadium. As if laying siege, the sky lit up with pulsing flashes of jagged bolts. We were in the last few minutes of a game that had already been decided. But in my humble opinion, it needed to be canceled. You know, like, *now*.

I glanced at Mike Webster, a Wisconsin farm boy who also knew the dangers of being caught outside in an electrical storm. He was looking rather uneasy and had taken to muttering to himself as we stood in the huddle. Looking intently at Mike, listening while he groused, I knew that I wasn't alone in cringing when it thundered, much less as the flash of lightning lit up the sky. The ingrained fears of my youth were sparking inside of me with every artillery outburst of electricity. And frankly, that's a bad choice of words: *sparking*. Especially when I remember that we were backed up toward our own end zone. That, of course, meant we were in the shadow of the goal post. Nothing like standing next to a giant lightning rod in the middle of a flat, wide-open area while huddling up with 10 other guys all wearing metal spikes. *Nothing to worry about at all, Wolf.* Looking around the huddle, from Tunch Ilkin to Mark Malone, the concern didn't seem to be affecting anyone else but Webbie and me.

As I said earlier, my father, Ron Wolfley, a Buffalo-born-and-bred truck driver, put the fear of lightning into me years before. And considering our family history, he had every reason. In fact, if Wolfley family history has proven anything, it's that we might be walking, talking human lightning rods. As a teenager working on my uncle's dairy farm, my dad got knocked off his feet from an indirect lightning strike. Seriously. Some of those big, old-fashioned milk cans on the milk truck were hit, and my dad was close enough to do a bug zapper impression. *Kaboom!*

My dad never forgot it, never got over it, and never let his kids forget it either. When the skies would darken anywhere in western New York, and rumblings started to roll through the heavens, my dad would make a mad dash to collect the kids. He made sure everybody skedaddled into the house before slamming the windows shut and battening down the hatches, baby. We had no air-conditioning, but that mattered little.

And then there's the story of my dad's grandfather, who had twin babies; well, one of those babies died from a lightning strike. You can maybe begin to understand the inbred fear that runs through the Wolfleys.

But wait, there's more! My older sister, Linrae, had a lightning bolt strike her umbrella while walking home one rainy day. She came through relatively unscathed, only a tad rattled. Thank God. And then there's my niece Amy. She endured an indirect lightning strike too. Still, as far as I know, my great-grandfather's baby is the only casualty.

All I knew standing out there on the field at Riverfront was that I didn't want to become one of them. There was no reason to take unnecessary chances. We had a big lead, the game was virtually over, and we only had to kneel on the ball a couple, three times. Maybe. End of story...or should've been.

Ahhh, good, here comes the rain. Perfect. Nothing like adding a little more electrical conductivity to the elements. Sheesh, I was beginning to feel like I was in one of those horror movies—you know, where you know something bad is coming but nobody else seems to be aware. Nobody except you and Mike Webster.

Mike was muttering louder now. He had a habit of coming into the locker room each week with what we used to refer to as the Mike Webster Daily Disaster Report. Somehow Mike would find out about disasters that occurred around the world and then tell everybody about them. Mudslides over in Indonesia, planes going down in China, avalanches in Alaska...whatever made the papers, Mike would find out and then dutifully report his findings. Sometimes he would share at the worst moments—like, you know, just before takeoff, or while we were in the air flying to a game, that sort of thing. In all fairness, I wasn't a nervous flyer until I started flying with Mike.

The rain slightly picked up in intensity and the skies continued to thunder. The referee put a towel over the ball as he stood over it at the line of scrimmage. Meanwhile, I was getting edgier and edgier. I walked to the line, up to the ref, and pointed out the obvious. He laughed, looking at me with the smug, sanctimonious look of someone who didn't know Ron Wolfley. He didn't know that we Wolfleys metabolically attracted lightning strikes like offensive linemen attract buffets.

People like that tick me off. Like Tunch. He loves thunderstorms. The goofball was actually hiking one time out West, with his sons Tanner and Clay. They were on top of a mountain in Montana, so high that the clouds were below them. In the distance a thunderstorm was brewing. Fascinated, he just hung out, watching the impending storm roll in. That is, until his boy Clay—rightly so, I might add—pointed out that it was an electrical storm, and getting caught on top of a mountain in a thunderstorm was a good way to die. *Oops.* Think about it. Tunch could have Darwined himself and the Ilkin clan right out of existence at that moment if his sons hadn't been smarter than their old man.

I turned to the official and reminded him that the game was, for all intents and purposes, over. I also reminded him that as the head ball ref in charge, he had the authority to call the game and get us off this potential field of death before something bad happened. He looked at me and laughed, and with a smile said, "You're not afraid of a little lightning, now, are you?"

At this point I was as jumpy as a three-pack-a-day smoker on cold turkey, day two. *Crack, boom!* More bolts and fireworks from above. I winced more outwardly than I wanted to, and the ref smirked yet again. I was trying to maintain my composure, but it was quickly crumbling. And that self-righteous smirk from the zebra got me. One more flash from overhead and I snapped. I moved in close and explained to him, in slightly heated terms, the Wolfley family history of getting lit up like Christmas trees—that it was in the DNA, that there had been at least three of us that we knew of who'd been bug-zapped.

Just then it boomed, and then flashed in jagged streaks. Then I pulled out my last stop. I moved closer and asked if he wanted a hug.

"Get away from me!" the ref said, a flash of sudden fear in his voice.

For the record, he didn't call the game early, and we won. Better yet, nobody got fried. And I *still* hate lightning.

CHAPTER 19

EYE IN THE SKY

They were the best of times; they were the worst of times.

Film review. After a win, sitting in there with the rest of the O-line can be glorious. Maybe you had some great earhole shots on a guy. Maybe you served up a pancake or two on a run play. Or maybe you wired a notable pass rusher all game long or even body-slammed him. Those are the days you really look forward to film review. And when you have an O-line coach who celebrates the big shots and physical play, it creates an atmosphere of guys hungry to get on the big screen for everyone to see.

Now, other days, well...

What needs to be understood is that after a normal Sunday game we would meet as a team on Tuesday. We always had the day after a game off. For those who were nicked or injured, that was a day to report for treatment. But if you came through the game relatively unscathed, you could stay in bed.

So on a typical Tuesday, everybody hit the Three Rivers Stadium parking lot about 9:00 in the morning. After meeting with Coach Noll as a team and then watching special teams together in the main meeting room, we would break off into our individual meeting groups. After the individual film review was complete, we would have to do some sort of running and lifting. But the film review was the big emphasis of the day. And depending on the result of the game two days before there was a varying degree of tension that built before we separated into the individual classrooms. Mike Webster, ever with the perfect pitch, once remarked, "Let's get to the rat killing, boys."

Watching game film is a yin-and-yang type of thing. There are always some good plays you want to see, and then there are those from which you wish you could hide. And then there are the plays you're not sure about. Picture it: You're sitting in front of your coaches and peers being critiqued a mere 48 hours after a game. And believe me, *nothing* is overlooked, unless you're a living legend. The Joe Greenes, the Mike

Websters, the Jack Lamberts, they would get the hall pass. The caustic remarks and hard coaching so typical back in the day were limited to us lesser mortals.

Being lambasted certainly did take some getting used to, especially when you had one of those games in which *everything* seemed to go wrong. Then you really needed to develop some thick skin, even mental armor. You had to learn to have an ear for what you did right and not let the criticism get to you personally. Otherwise, it could wear on you. Part of the problem was the anticipation of getting reamed out for a bad play, series, or game that put you in a sweat. And let's not underestimate the very real threat of unemployment. Too many bad days at Black Rock, and that was a real possibility. It hung over your head like the sword of Damocles.

One of the hallmarks of Chuck Noll's coaching was his ability to make us compete day in and day out for our jobs. Or at least make you feel like you were. This was before free agency and such made playing in the 1980s and 1990s, as I did, seem like medieval times. So there you were, sitting in a group of your peers, alongside guys such as Jon Kolb, Mike Webster, Larry Brown—legends, guys you wanted to emulate, guys you respected and wanted to respect you, guys whose level you wanted to rise to. I mean, those guys were tough, physical, extraordinary men who set a standard in the room. Their physically dominant style of play was applauded by coaches and teammates alike. So naturally you wanted to be tough and physical like them. You wanted to put some pancakes up on the screen and hear their *oohs* and *ahs*.

Regardless of the outcome of a game, you always had a reel of bad plays looping in your head. It was a reel that would keep me tossing and turning at night. I remember watching the sun come up after playing on *Monday Night Football*, unable to fall asleep in my lounge chair, running plays over and over in my head. It might only be three or four bummer plays out of 60 to 80, but those three or four would loop endlessly.

Getting to and through film review was the best antidote to a poor game or loss. It was like purging all your crimes and misdemeanors, or atoning after confession. Plus, even if you made a good play, there was a strong chance that your position coach was still pissed off and might not even comment on it.

Once, after a loss out West against the Seahawks, I blocked down on the nose tackle and mulched him. I got into him deep and kept driving my legs. I must've driven him a dozen yards off the line of scrimmage and buried him into the turf. In my mind, I was thinking, *C'mon, Rollie! Give me a little shot here, would ya?* Bubkes. Nothing but stony silence. But back in the '80s, mulching, powerful hits, and slobberknockers were the currency of close-quarters combat in the trenches. But a little coaching appreciation went a long way, to be sure.

Mike Webster once shared with me the best advice on how to keep from having your confidence destroyed. He said to take the positive stuff and learn from it, but let the rest "flow like water off a duck's butt." *OL Zen for Idiots*, right? But Webbie was absolutely right. Of course, he was the best center to ever play the game, so I'm not sure that he ever really had any bad ones. It was extremely rare for Mike to grade out lower than the 92nd percentile. He was just that good. Me, on the other hand? I experienced a few of those rough days. They come with the job description. Being a human crash test dummy has its ups and downs, and it's certainly not for everybody.

There are also the funny moments that come from the "eye in the sky that don't lie." It wasn't always "doom and gloom in the room," as someone once put it. We were playing the Miami Dolphins one year. Tyrone McGriff, a teammate and fellow rookie guard, also a starter in that rookie year, pulled out to lead on an off-tackle play. Vern Den Herder, a grizzled and wizened vet playing the defensive end position in the Miami 3-4, played over the top on a down block. Literally, as the tight end tried to drive him inside, Den Herder played across the face of the tight end and tried to get to the outside rather than penetrate up the field. In doing so, Vern started to fall, and upon falling quickly attempted to roll over in an effort to throw his body into the hole. Remember, this was at a time when the phrase "making business decisions" wasn't in anyone's mind. Those didn't exist. This was an era when no one was worried about his own safety, or anyone else's, for that matter.

Tyrone, pulling around the outside, turned up into the hole just as Den Herder fell. Vern just threw himself into the hole as he was falling to try to stack some bodies. While whirling, falling, and trying to make some semblance of a play, ol' Vern whipped his arm around in a windmilling motion, mindlessly trying to hit whoever, wherever, however, he could. Well, it was a one-in-a-million shot where he landed—point blank in Tyrone's groin as he was pulling around the corner. And it was a particularly wicked shot.

Ouch. *Big* ouch. Back then, guys only wore a jock strap; not too many wore a cup. It was more of a hindrance than a necessity. So when you got a direct shot, you wished you *did* wear one. We watched that play over and over. Everybody groaned in unison in empathy for Tyrone. Rollie replayed it in fast motion and then in slow motion. Man, it was hilarious. After that initial groan, everyone began to laugh as the play was repeated. Well, everybody but poor Tyrone. Still, his reaction—and the fact that it was captured on film—well, it was priceless.

For some reason the camera kept running and stayed focused on Tyrone after the play was over. Tyrone immediately reacted to the groin shot by grabbing himself in the tenderized area, crouching down and curling up protectively. He then began alternating between standing up to angrily point to Den Herder and resuming the fetal position as another wave of pain and nausea swept over him. The referee didn't seem to understand poor Tyrone as he continually alternated between the standing and fetal positions several times over, going into the squat position and then making angry gestures toward the amused Den Herder,

Making my bones on tape against the great Art Still. Courtesy of the Pittsburgh Steelers

who stood on the Miami side of the ball looking at McGriff and acting as if he didn't know what happened.

Those are the things you remember so many years down the road. The eye in the sky, run by longtime Steelers film chief Bob McCartney, captured a lot of things post-play that could be filed as unusual. We used to play at the old Cleveland Municipal Stadium before the Browns left town. It was a real rock pile, home of the infamous Dawg Pound. The stadium was demolished in November 1996, and I said good riddance to the worst outdoor stadium of the 20th century.

But one of those unusual moments picked up on film occurred there back in the early 1980s. We played preseason games with Cleveland in addition to our two regular-season games. There was a security guard who used to sit on a folding chair just below the scoreboard, which was at field level, probably 10 yards or so behind the end zone. It sat 15 to 20 feet in the air. The camera would quickly flash to the scoreboard to show the down, distance, and time clock before each play, and you would see this elderly gentleman just sitting there, scratching, picking his nose, whatever. It really was funny since he didn't know he was being filmed. Our line coach—the Big Kahuna, Ron Blackledge, who took over for Dotsch my third year with the Steelers—always said he was going to put in for the security guard's job whenever his coaching days were over.

Ron was a very successful coach who spent 33 years in the coaching ranks—nine seasons at the high school level in Canton, Ohio; 14 in college; and 14 in the NFL. He often said the key to coaching success was to only unpack half the moving boxes in your garage. Anyway, a few years down the road, we were saddened to learn that the old security guard was no longer there. And the Big Kahuna never did get the job because the stadium was mercifully demolished.

But back to the film room. Having to watch a play unfold when you were run over or physically beaten was torturous. I absolutely *hated* it. All linemen do. It's one thing to have a mental error, or miss a guy, but to actually get freight-trained? Well, it would leave you with some sleepless nights before film day. Remember, offensive linemen don't score touchdowns, or celebrate sacks, or make spectacular catches. We celebrated big hits. Crunches. Pancakes. Those made your reputation. And in the blood-sport world inside the trenches, reputation is everything.

You wanna make your bones? Do it against the best, because that's where reputations are handed out. Try and pancake a Randy White, a Reggie White, a Kevin Greene, a Lawrence Taylor. Stuff a "Too Tall" Jones, a John Matuszak, a Joe Klecko, a Rulon Jones, a Michael Dean Perry. Try to run over a Mike Singletary, a Clay Matthews, a Randy Gradishar, a Ronnie Lott. *That's* how you stand out. That's how you find your place in the world of alpha male trench fighters. It's a tough world in between the tackles, not for the faint of heart. And it all plays out in the classroom in film review each and every week. It's always there. As Mike Tomlin says, it's your résumé.

There's an old saying, "Winning covers up a lot of sins." When we won the game, we would get a little more clemency for "indiscretions." But when we lost, you knew those suspect plays were coming up during film review. You couldn't help yourself. You squirmed in your chair as if you had ants in your pants.

These days, Coach Tomlin collects a number of plays that he finds highly suspect—guys getting beat, putting in poor effort, etc.—and puts them all together on one video for the whole team called *The News*. It's a highlight film that you don't want to be part of. And as Mike T says, "I don't make the news. I just report it."

Well, I would've made the news back in the early 1980s when we were playing the Houston Oilers in the old Astrodome. I became a starter my second year, and one of the defensive tackles playing for the Oilers was a third-year guy named Mike Stensrud, out of Iowa. Mike was a big guy, 6'5", 315 pounds. There weren't as many 300-pounders back in the day, but Mike was all of that and probably more. Anyway, on a passing down, the defensive tackle over me came on a pass rush, rushing hard to the inside between me and Mike Webster. I punched my man in his shoulders, locked out my arms while sliding down hip-to-hip with Webbie, and passed my man off to him. It's always important to remain uniform, stay hip-to-hip, and stay square in the inner-three triangle of both guards setting with the center. Penetration kills the run game, but penetration in the passing game gets quarterbacks mangled.

There's another old saying, specifically for the trenches: "Something going away; something coming back." You didn't get complacent just because you'd passed your man off to someone else on a stunt because there was a very good chance something or somebody was coming back at you. "Something wicked this way comes" were words to live by. So I punched off my man to Mike, slid down to protect his hip, and sank back slightly to check on what was happening with Jon Kolb, our left tackle. Jon was locked in mortal combat all day long with noted head-slapper and bell-ringer Elvin Bethea. Bethea was a terrific defensive end for the Oilers, and Kolb's battles with Elvin over the years were the stuff of legend. Elvin was in his 15th year at this point, and Kolb was in his 13th. The two of them had been going at it twice a year for more than a decade, so if familiarity bred contempt, they were contempt's poster children.

Suddenly, coming around the corner, I caught a hard-charging rhino at full gallop. All 315 pounds (and probably 20 more not listed) of full-throttle Stensrud impaled me, his helmet crashing into my chest as I missed my punch over the top of his shoulder pads. You want to talk about being in a bad position? This was a very poor one, folks.

The Oilers were running what we used to call a Tom game. A Tom game was a twist stunt by the two inside defensive tackles. One would be the penetrator and the other the looper, or the guy who trailed on the pass-rush stunt. The penetrator would try to get into the gap between two offensive linemen and create a break in the wall of protection. If the penetrator got up the field into the gap, you would have a jailbreak. The two offensive linemen would be forced into fighting against each other as the penetrator got up the field. And while you were trying to stop the penetrator, the looper would come on the twist with a full head of steam. If you weren't aware, or didn't have your eyes or radar on the action around you, you could end up being railroaded by a guy who could drive you into the quarterback. It was the ultimate humiliation for an offensive lineman.

The great Steelers tackle Larry Brown once told me that he used to keep a picture of Terry Bradshaw lying on the ground, with Larry lying on his back on top of him, and the Bills defensive end Ben Williams on top them both. Years later, whenever he began to miss football, he would pull out that picture to remind himself why he was glad he was retired. After looking at it, Bubba said he didn't miss football at all!

With experience, linemen learn to develop a samurai sixth sense in pass protection. With all the different stunts and twists that a defense can throw at you, constantly roving your eyes and listening to the little survival voices that game repetitions develop, you grow into a battle-hardened veteran over the years. But when the wildebeest named Stensrud came flying around the corner, being a young guy, I had neither my eyes nor my radar fully operational at that time. Oh, baby, he hit me like a locomotive! It was a staggering, full-on bull rush with a head-snapping, spine-crackling hit that only Wile E. Coyote could appreciate.

Mike hit me so forcefully, so hard, all I could do was try to stay upright, on my feet, and in front of the car crash in which I was currently engaged. So quickly did he hit me, and with such speed, that I was literally running backward like a cartoon character. To be honest, I thought just staying upright on my feet was one heckuva job well-done by me. But things got worse.

Stensrud drove me straight back 10 yards. Yes, 10 full yards. I know this because Webbie counted them out loud while we watched the film two days later. And if you ran the film in reverse, it looked like I was trying to catch a cab with long strides at full speed. Stensrud had so much momentum that we roared past Bradshaw. As a matter of fact, Mike didn't even see Terry because his helmet was buried in my chest. Terry had taken a five-step drop on the pass, and my current dance partner and I blew by him without so much as an outstretched hand from Stensrud. When we finally came to a halt, Mike actually had to turn and run back toward the line of scrimmage to get after Bradshaw, who had barely even noticed the Wolfley-Stensrud Express blowing by him. It would have easily been the most humiliating sack I ever allowed had Stensrud actually slowed down enough to see the QB.

At film review, I cringed in the dark as the play approached. Now, there's another old saying: "You never play as poorly as you think, and you never play as well as you think." That was my hope.

Nope. This was bad. In the dark I could hear Rollie Dotsch clear his throat. I knew he was going to rip me. Rollie was a tough, old-school guy who was as hard on rookies as he had advertised before the start of training camp.

That speech went like this: "Guys, you're bottom-feeders, the lowest life form in camp. I promise you, I will be hard on you. You might make the exact same mistake a veteran does, and I won't say a word to them but I will be all over you. They've earned their spurs. You haven't."

Given that, I expected the full brunt of Rollie's wrath, if it was as bad as I remembered. Rollie was silent as the play unfolded on the big screen. I could hear the hum of the 16mm projector, feel the inescapable shame of having a roomful of tough guys see when you are physically beaten. Sweat collected around the collar of my shirt. Privately, I was praying that the film would break, or that maybe a sinkhole would open up under my feet and swallow me. The room felt uncomfortably warm. Snickers arose in the darkened room as Rollie replayed my hood-ornament moment.

"I didn't know you could run backward that fast," Rollie quipped. "Did you get the license plate number?" This is about the only printable version I can offer. Suffice it to say, his reaction was as toxic, ripping, and hard-nosed as I could have anticipated. And the words are worse when spoken in the acid-tinged tone of an old-school coach like Rollie. The real translation: "There better not be another of those anytime soon, if you want to stay employed."

Yet nobody could make you more uncomfortable than Coach Noll. He had the ability, as Tunch Ilkin once said, "to give you a look that could make you lose bladder control." In my rookie year we played in the old Metropolitan Stadium against the Vikings. It couldn't have been too late in the season because it wasn't that cold. I was playing on special teams—and I had a pretty good game, at least in my own mind.

On punt return, I lined up on the guard, but I was to pick up R-3, the third man right of center. Trust me, I was kicking his butt. I actually drove him into the backfield and mulched him on the ground once.

I didn't even let him cross the line of scrimmage. It was almost too easy. But our unit wasn't getting the job done, and nobody could put their finger on why. Still, I had some pretty good blocks, and my coverage on both kickoff and punt were all good.

So on Tuesday, when we sat down as a group to watch the special teams reel, I was feeling upbeat and eagerly anticipated the film. Coach Noll was the special teams coach then. He was very particular about coaching the unit; it was his personal baby. So I felt he would like my ground-and-pound on the one return. We came to the first punt return and I'm drilling my man, R-3, but R-2 was running free down the field and creamed the return man. Chuck didn't say anything at first, but I was thinking, *Come on, Coach. I had a pretty good hit!*

Then, as if answering my mental telepathy, Coach Noll, in an aggravated voice, said, "Wolfley, what man do you have on this middle return?" The hum of the projector as Coach kept running it forward and backward made enough noise to cover my stuttering. Middle? I thought it was a right return. *Oh no.* I was desperately searching my mind, but as the film played out, everybody else was blocking for a middle return. I was the only man on a right return. I was blocking R-3 when I should've been blocking R-2.

My mouth's moisture had suddenly evaporated and my brain had turned to mush. "Ummm...ahhh...duh, dub, errr...ahhh" was about all I could muster. I couldn't utter anything remotely comprehensible. The buzz from the projector rolled on, providing the only solace and noise cover for me. I suddenly realized what lay ahead of me. And it was not good.

Mike Tomlin has said he doesn't have a doghouse. Fine. But believe me, Coach Noll definitely did. And I was about to check in to it for a while. I was considering getting cable TV installed too.

Somebody throw me a bone, please?

It gets worse. The second and the third punt returns were almost identical. I'm drilling my man, it's a middle return, and again I'm whaling on R-3 while R-2 is free-ranging and crushing our punt returner. Coach doesn't say squat. My mental error was out there for everybody to see. After the third one resulted in another crushing hit on our return man, I could feel the heat coming from Coach. In fact, I was sitting in a Turkish steam bath. Coach Noll just shut off the projector, and there was a mausoleum-at-midnight-quality darkness in the main meeting room. During the hush the proverbial pin dropped. All the veterans in the room seemingly inhaled as one, knowing what was coming. There were nearly 60 people sitting in this meeting room, but it was quieter than a Plymouth Brethren prayer meeting.

"Wolfley, just what do you do during the special teams meeting?" The words hung in the air like a bomb waiting to drop on me. This was not a friendly tone, folks. This was panic city. Coach Noll, being the special teams coach, took great pride in everybody knowing, doing, and executing his assignment. It was very personal with Coach when you screwed yours up.

My mind raced, trying to come up with a suitable answer. But since I'm the only moron running a right return while everybody else was running a middle return, there was no one else to blame but me. And at the moment, nothing even remotely semi-intelligible came to mind. I was bearing the full brunt of the fury that only a Chuck Noll nonverbal communication could deliver.

Silence. Tick...tick...tick.

Just when I thought he was going to explode, Coach said in an icy tone, "Pay attention."

Silence. More silence. Then, the projector started chattering away. And the entire room breathed again.

CHAPTER 20

THE BIG RAGU

Training camp is unlike anything that a normal person, at least outside of the military, encounters. Of course, I'm *not* comparing football camp with those who survive Parris Island or any other military boot camp. Sure, they share some things in common, but after watching my son go through Ranger School and seeing the emaciated young man who emerged from that trial, I can say that I had never been to the edge of myself like he had. Not even the infamous Purge of '84 training camp, when Chuck Noll decided to clean house, can compare. Coach was determined to forge a team in the fires of a ridiculously fierce training camp in Latrobe. (That was the year Franco Harris ended up in Seattle.)

But pain *is* a common denominator in both football and the military, and a Noll training camp was always a foray into pain. Chuck repeatedly reminded us we had to will our bodies to get it done. Another Noll-ism was, "You have to know the difference between pain and injury."

A Chuck Noll camp was never about making the team; it was always about surviving the moment. Put enough moments together, and then—and only then—would you worry about making the team. Survival was job number one, and with that came a high attrition rate. Guys would often disappear in the middle of the night—just up and leave. So we had guys who were signed to fill out roster spots in camp; we called them "campers." In those years, teams would enlist over 100 guys to begin training camp. You would know, and most of them knew, that they had little chance of making the team. But with two practices a day, full go with full pads, you needed the bodies. And without the NFL Players Association protections that limit full contact today, injuries were rampant. There was a saying back in the day: "Open up a new can of player and add water."

The practices were brutal, and the conditions in camp weren't much better. Among the other factors that led to attrition were dorm life (no air-conditioning and horse-hair-stuffed mattresses); the food (God bless the nuns up at camp, but cooking wasn't exactly their forte); and homesickness (Andy Russell told the story of being at camp for nine weeks). Whatever the reason, guys got gone, never to be seen again.

I can remember more than once, sitting in the team meeting room up at St. Vincent College sweating to death in full pads (there was never a day wearing anything less) before heading out for the first practice of the day. Looking around, you might notice the team was down a man or two. And being down a man meant a heavier workload for everybody else.

One time a player was bent on leaving and, lacking a ride, packed up his stuff and walked through the cornfields to get to Arnold Palmer Airport. There are always funny moments at training camp. Things that weren't necessarily funny become funny in the rearview mirror, like that guy. But this next story was definitely funny then, funny in the rearview mirror, and is still hilarious today.

It involves one of my favorite modern-era players, a guy who belongs in the Legacy of the 73ers: the guys who've worn the No. 73 throughout their careers, including me, Kendall Simmons, and of course, the Big Ragu, Ramon Foster. I was a broadcaster then, and I happened, naturally, to be hanging around the offensive linemen, mentally taking notes, getting a grip on the newbies, and checking on the technique du jour on this very hot day. I watched the hogs going through their individual period; there's always something to pick up in technique or scheme if you pay attention.

The line coach under Mike Tomlin at the time was Larry Zierlein, and he had chosen to work on the cut block, which is a difficult block to practice. The cut block, or chop block, involves an offensive lineman simply going airborne commando at a man, throwing his body, and trying to take the defender off his feet. Former Steelers guard and Super Bowl champ (and recent Hall of Honor recipient) Gerry "Moon" Mullins was exceptional at this technique. He even acquired the nickname Chopper because of his ability to get guys on the ground in the open field. You might even catch Moon in action in a Super Bowl highlight replay with a beautiful cut block on Vikings OLB Wally Hilgenberg while leading Franco Harris around the corner.

These days, much hand-wringing has been spent on trying to eliminate the cut block due to its high propensity to injure players; it's especially hard on the knee joints. Even practicing the block on a full-go day is verboten. The solution is to take one of those pop-up bags that are about four feet tall, with a weighted bottom. The bag will stand upright and automatically pop back up after someone crushes it to the ground. You can throw the cross-body block at the bag and learn the technique without blowing out anyone's knee. It's not exactly the same as using a human body, but frankly, would *you* like to stand there and have a massive, 300-plus-pound monster running at you and throwing his body at your legs? *Thank you, but I'll pass.*

So we're there in practice. Max Starks, Willie Colon, and Chris Kemoeatu all took their turns nailing the bag and making a giant *whomp* sound after crushing it to the ground. Each successive rep was met with a quick review by Zierlein. As the O-line coach, Larry was all about talking through the keys to a good cut block: things like approaching under control, driving through the outside leg of the defender while punching through with the inside arm, stuff like that.

And then came the Big Ragu, all 350 pounds of legitimate tough guy. He was just a kid at the time, an undrafted free agent. He wasn't just a camp body, though, because the Steelers had a draftable grade on the young man. There was hope, and he was full of vim and vigor, to say the least. Foster accelerated five to six steps, gathered slightly, and then went airborne, headfirst, aiming for the bag and intent on making a monstrous hit with that monstrous body.

Everything looked great. Foster was laid out, looking aerodynamically sound, even. I was watching a first-rate cross-body block on an inanimate object. I mean, how could you miss? Except...he did.

The Big Ragu, Ramon Foster (left), wore the same No. 73 and played the same left guard position for the Steelers as I did. Courtesy of the Pittsburgh Steelers

Say what?

Yep. Literally a swing and a miss. In all my years, I had *never* seen a whiff of this magnitude. The resounding *whomp* sound that had come with the preceding players' reps was replaced by a ginormous *thunk* sound when the massive 350-pound junkyard dog, Foster, crashed to Mother Earth.

I turned to Tunch Ilkin and said simply, "Did I just see what I think I saw?" I started to laugh in disbelief. Tunch was incredulous his laughter and puzzlement confirmed it. He spoke in a stunned voice, as if he were reporting a UFO sighting. And that begat *more* laughter. Not from Tunch or me. Oh no, we were already among a chorus of guffaws reacting to the ridiculousness of what we had just seen. Huge, deep, resoundingly loud laughter came from Ramon's peer group.

After boning himself in the failed cut block attempt, Ramon quickly got back to his feet with a quizzical, embarrassed look on his face. Tunch was no help because he had a belly laugh going comparable to mine. And we didn't have a corner on the hysterics. It was all around us in the guys watching and Larry Zierlein. They were all laughing uproariously.

There was no way to talk your way out of this one. The boys saw it, the sideline noncombatants such as Tunch and I saw it. Fans on the hill who were paying attention to a rather mundane drill saw it. And I believe there was a trainer or two in the neighborhood who saw the whole thing too.

Foster had just pulled off the one thing that you would think he couldn't possibly do: catch a down draft while hurling himself at the bag and pancaking himself with a complete whifferrooski. *Oh, you had to be there.*

How I wish I could have sat in the meeting room that night with the hogs while they reviewed the film. I mean, there had to be some video confirmation of the worst cut block in the history of the Pittsburgh Steelers. Of course, I say that with all the love in my heart for Ramon, who did indeed go on to make the team. In fact, the Big Ragu was one of the best and toughest players to ever play for the Steelers.

CHAPTER 21

BIG RED HEADS TO CANTON

I can't tell you how happy I was for Alan Faneca—along with his lovely wife, Julie, and the entire Faneca clan—when he was inducted into the Pro Football Hall of Fame in 2021. It was way past time for Alan to get his gold jacket and line up alongside the other Hall of Famers, for him to rightly be acclaimed in the Valhalla Hall of heavy hitters and be enshrined as a member of that very exclusive club.

I remember when the Steelers drafted him. It was way back in 1998, in the first round of the draft. He went on to play 10 seasons with the Steelers and 13 overall in the NFL. He and Jeff Hartings were the leaders up front for the Super Bowl XL team that won in Detroit seven seasons after he was drafted. Faneca was selected to nine Pro Bowls and named All-Pro six times. He was also named to the Steelers' All-Time Team in 2007. And let's not forget that he was named to the NFL All-Decade Team for the 2000s.

So yeah, it was a disappointment that he was passed over in Hall of Fame voting five times. Five times he was snubbed! Maybe "Steelers fatigue" was a real deal. At least it looked that way to me. Then again, it's my biased opinion that the Steelers should have their own wing in the Hall. (And by the way, I've been in the Hall of Fame room of busts after hours, and John Madden was right: they *do* talk to each other.)

It's high time to give Alan's tenure here in Pittsburgh the kudos it deserves and highlight all the accolades that have followed Big Red throughout his fabulous career. Unlike other positions, being an offensive lineman is, first and foremost, an exercise in humility. There are no career stats that can comparatively rate you among the brotherhood of pancakers—just height and weight, games played, games started, Pro Bowls… those sorts of things. Sure, you can talk about the bench press. Or about how much they can eat, but even skinny guys can eat; one time I saw the late, great L. C. Greenwood work on three or four different plates of steak, eggs, pancakes, and other assorted "fooditives" a mere four or five hours before kickoff. A very impressive effort for a skinny guy, sayeth this fat guy.

But for offensive linemen, there are no 100-yard rushing accolades, no scoring touchdowns, interceptions, passing percentage stats, or the like, so it's difficult to be compared to others. As a matter of fact, the less you hear an offensive lineman's name, the better, because when you do, it's because of a penalty being blared over the stadium PA system, or a TV analyst talking about who gave up the sack.

For me, legendary hits are the barometer. For nearly 40 years I've been privileged to have a front-row seat to some of the greatest slobberknockers in Steelers history, either on the field or from the sideline. And let me tell you, *nobody* does it like the fat guys up front.

I was fortunate enough to watch the legendary Larry Brown make two—not one, but two—different defensive ends actually quit rushing the passer for an entire game. They instead spent the afternoon playing the draw or screen pass rather than going after the QB because neither one of those ends wanted any more to do with Boss Brown, as we called him. They waved the white flag of surrender on pass plays after they were nailed early in the game with a couple of Larry's howitzer punches to the chest. In fairness, there's something about having your sternum touch your spine that makes the prospect of getting hit there again so unappealing. Those volcanic punches were fueled by the ginormous guns Larry sported back in the day. When Boss Brown walked into a room, it was said his triceps entered five minutes later. He was the guy on game day.

Then there was Steve Courson, who launched the Raiders' Jack Tatum and one-hopped him to the bench after an interception by Tatum at Three Rivers Stadium. Once, Courson made Bengals OLB Reggie Williams do a backflip, he hit him so hard. Williams looked like one of those dudes running from the bulls in Pamplona, Spain. And this bull won.

Mike Webster broke the will, and nearly the back, of Cincinnati nose tackle Wilson Whitley with just sheer, overwhelming, muscular power.

The granite-jawed Jon Kolb was so strong and powerful he won the NFL's Strongest Man contest. He used that strength to crumple the real Darth Vader of the NFL, Lyle Alzado, on a run play.

Tunch Ilkin once overpowered and slammed Giants Hall of Famer Lawrence Taylor to the ground so hard and viciously that he was flagged for holding. He was howling at the ref in the huddle, and the ref told him, "You had to be holding. Nobody throws L.T. down like that without holding him." (Seriously. I was standing next to Chalooch in the huddle and heard it.)

From flashback to flash forward, there was the Big Ragu, Ramon Foster, pancaking former Ravens linebacker C. J. Mosley—one of the most explosive, dynamic hits I've ever seen. Foster trucked Mosley and virtually vaporized the man. Picture an 18-wheeler running over a Volkswagen Beetle. These are the hits that define offensive linemen. These are the hits that give a little insight into those players' greatness.

I remember watching from the sideline when Faneca pulled around on a trap block and went face mask–to–face mask with a Bengals linebacker. Alan hit this guy so hard the linebacker's helmet shot straight up in the air like the head on a Rock 'Em Sock 'Em Robot. I'm telling you, that helmet went at least two feet in the air, as if somebody had popped it like a zit. I've never seen that happen before or since.

I also remember the time Faneca was rolling in the open field with a back carrying the rock behind him. Alan hit a linebacker so hard, the 'backer went down on his keister, did a backward roll, and came to his feet, only to be steamrolled a second time by the hard-charging Faneca. Two pancake blocks on the same guy in one play. I shook my head in disbelief. But Alan regularly turned linebackers into crash test dummies.

And who can forget Faneca leading Willie Parker on a Boss play and splatting poor Lofa Tatupu, the unfortunate Seattle linebacker. He mulched Tatupu, and Parker took off for the longest rushing touchdown in Super Bowl history.

Wolf List: My Top 10 Greatest Opponents

There are so many formidable guys that I played with during my career, mentioning them all could fill another book in itself. Teammate or opponent, these are the 10 best I ever squared off against in the NFL.

10. Dan Hampton
9. Marty Lyons
8. Clyde Simmons
7. Lyle Alzado
6. William "the Refrigerator" Perry
5. Curley Culp
4. Matt Millen
3. Lawrence Taylor
2. Randy "Slayer" White
1. Joe Greene

Don't forget about the time the Steelers were forced by injuries to shuttle Faneca from guard to tackle on obvious third-down passing situations. That modification allowed the Steelers to adequately protect Ben Roethlisberger. Alan said after that game that playing tackle was a lot easier than playing guard, and that those highly paid tackles were "stealing money."

For the rest of us schlubs, an afternoon of pass blocking out at the offensive tackle position is a foray into pain. It's just not quite so easy. But it was easy—easy for him. Easy if you're a Hall of Famer. Which Faneca is. Forever.

So I give a belated congratulations to one of the greatest players in the history of the NFL, and more importantly, one of the greatest Steelers ever to wear the Black and Gold.

Alan Faneca. Hall of Famer. Class of 2021.

CHAPTER 22

BUSINESS DECISIONS

One of the newer and more overused expressions that's emerged in recent years in the NFL is "business decision." Not in calculating the cap or researching the latest, greatest Color Rush uniform variation. Not deciding where to send two NFL teams overseas in an effort to broaden the NFL's marketing appeal, or even how to prepare for collective bargaining talks. Nope, I'm talking business decisions as in deciding when, how, and where to engage on the field of play.

A business decision is made when a player questions whether or not he is going to put his body at risk. The code of honor says you lay it on the line all the time. That's the way the game was played in my day. If you didn't, you would've been mocked. But that was back in the day. Understand, I'm talking about players here, not specialists like kickers or punters. Theirs are business decisions that are expected.

A friend of mine relayed a conversation he had with a player from another team. The player was asked how he kept himself in shape and how he has sustained relatively few injuries during the course of his double-digit-year NFL career. "I make business decisions on the field," he said. *I kid you not.*

Now, I don't know if that player really understood the significance of what he said, or how it sounded when it tumbled from his brain and out of his mouth like a gumball from a machine. But as a player from the days of yore, someone from the dark ages of the NFL, when trolls, dragons, orcs, and elves battled in Middle Earth, I can say definitively that it left me shaking my head. Business decisions!

I don't think guys like Bronko Nagurski, Dick Butkus, Deacon Jones, and Joe Greene would understand today's concept of the term, much less accept it. Obviously, the NFL is changing, unquestionably. And in most respects it's for the better, especially for the health of the guys, and by extension that of the game.

Yes, I get the lack of hitting during the season, particularly the fear of noggin damage—the worst of all the possible outcomes that could befall a player on any given Sunday. The watering down of violence in the game has unquestionably gone a long way to bettering the post-career prospects of the average ex-NFLer, who can live a fairly normal life. And certainly the financial windfall today's player enjoys soothes much of the aches and pains of participating in a career within what I think is the greatest sport in the world.

But when you refer to making "business decisions" in the game, deciding when to take on a trap block or when to take the easy way out and run around it, then I think we're starting to get to a point in time when the integrity of the game is being challenged. Let me make it clear: it's not the running around a block that concerns me. Shoot, there are plenty of guys who can run around a block and still make the play. It's the concept of not engaging for fear of injury that concerns me, the mindset of looking at yourself as a separate entity from that of your teammates and the color of your jersey. When a guy decides protecting himself is more important than leaving it all on the field, the sanctity of the team is damaged.

Maybe I'm being too harsh, too old-school, or just too old *period*, but there was a time in the league when laying it all on the line meant something, when "winning is everything" was really everything. There was a time when a man's honor on the field of play was his calling card, when playing the game the right way was bigger than the size of the paycheck. Okay, I was a bit of an extremist in that regard, I'll grant you. Most of us from back in the day were. The money wasn't big enough to overwhelm us. For us, it was about the pure love of the game.

Two-a-days, full pads, Astroturf, Oklahoma drills, live one-on-one pass rushes with nothing but shorts, T-shirts, and helmets. Yes, it was a harsh time in the NFL. But there was a purity about it too—something that's hard to convey to the young bucks today. To us it was about sacrifice, about the game being bigger than any one individual, and about us overcoming challenges as a team, not as a collection of individuals. It

Making so-called business decisions on the field of play was not part of my DNA.
Courtesy of the Pittsburgh Steelers

was about being a Steeler, pulling your weight, staying accountable to one another.

Ours was a brotherhood: the coming together before the game, the halftime adjustments, our families sitting in the stands…the "Pittsburgh Polka," for crying out loud. It was the prospect of the chaos, carnage, and sheer thrill of violence exploding around us that made our eyelids slam open when we woke up on game day. It was the heart-hammering rendition of the national anthem just prior to kickoff, the last headbutt with a teammate before taking the field for the first play of the game, the incredible rush of adrenaline you got looking into the eyes of future Hall of Famers—a Randy White, Reggie White, Lawrence Taylor, or Howie Long.

It was the magic of winning, the release of sitting in the Three Rivers Stadium sauna after a hard-fought battle. So many of us would be crammed into that wooden structure, with an adult beverage or two. We told the stories of the day, and maybe stretched the truth a little here and there, knowing full well the "eye in the sky that don't lie" truth detector would be in full force in the team meetings a mere 48 hours later.

Business decisions? The only business decisions we made after those games were which restaurant or whose house we were hitting after we got out of the sauna.

Business decisions? It was the wife pulling on your arm, telling you it's time to go, reminding you that the kids had school the next day.

Business decisions? Nope. The only business decision to be made at that point was, "Yes, dear, let's go home."

But, really, those were the only business decisions that had to be made. Back in the day.

CHAPTER 23

WHAT MAKES TROY, TROY?

In my nearly 40 years of playing, watching, living, and breathing Steelers football, no one has come close to matching the spectrum of talents exhibited by the flying Samoan human crash test dummy that is Troy Polamalu. And I say that with all the love and respect in the world for a very special man. On and off the field, Troy was special. Whether it was the hair, his Polynesian ancestry, or his friendly personality, it was easy to see that he was different.

There is a saying that strength is for service and service is for reaching out to those who are less fortunate. I don't think anyone manifested that truism better than Troy. Whether it was visiting Children's Hospital without any fanfare or press, or just taking the time to brighten the day of a special-needs child watching practice, Troy reached them by reaching out to them. He understood the power of touch, of human compassion.

Simply identifying the over-the-top, physical attributes of Troy is easy. He was gifted with great speed, close-quarter quickness, and a powerful body. He also possessed a competitive mind that fueled an incredible drive. He could play over-the-top coverage on the fastest of receivers, or go over the top of the line of scrimmage to defend a quarterback sneak. He was also "over-the-top" in diving to extend for the ball on an interception, or in going over the pylon for a touchdown to finish a return. Shoot, Troy even went over-the-top when he dove into the crowd during the victory parade following Super Bowl XLIII, leaping out of the car he was riding in.

Among his 783 tackles, his under-the-radar 56 tackles for loss were particularly outstanding. He also recorded 12 sacks in his 12-year career, the forerunner of today's version of the sub-package hybrid linebacker. He truly could do it all.

Sure, you could list the usual suspects when it came to his intangibles: drive, determination, leadership, a never-say-die attitude. But that merely scratches the surface. He was also humble, and in today's modern sports world, that is a rare commodity indeed. But his humility underscored everything he did. I mean, I still think you have to dig even deeper. The man was almost monastic in depth, persona, and conversation.

But on the field, he possessed great instinct, controlled aggression, and an almost uncanny ability to time the snap count. He had a unique ability to compute down, distance, and personnel, add scouting reports and film review, and dump it into an equation that made sense to him. The results of which equaled him coming up with a big play.

Obviously it all starts with his ridiculous athleticism. In my mind, that was the foundation that made Troy great. There would've been no eye-popping interceptions, sacks, fumble recoveries, forced fumbles, or returns for touchdowns had it not been for his overabundance of God-given quick-twitch muscle fibers. You could always tell when Troy hit max speed, because his hair would fly straight out like a flag blowing in the wind. But that's just stating the obvious. Gross motor skills, which an old offensive lineman such as me understands, are not to be confused with fine motor skills, things like hand-eye coordination.

When it came to interceptions and spectacular grabs, Troy was doing Odell Beckham Jr. before there was an OBJ. Think of the hand-eye coordination and vertical hops he displayed in coverage against WR Kenny Britt during Troy's memorable first quarter of the 2009 prime-time opener. I remember Troy leaping, high-pointing, and one-handing the deep pass to intercept Titans quarterback Kerry Collins. Or if you're looking for the more horizontal variety of sensational, how about Troy laying out and scooping a ball off the turf with one hand to rob Philip Rivers and the San Diego Chargers in 2008?

How about the closing speed Troy exhibited in coming out of nowhere to take down Titans roadrunner RB Chris Johnson in that same Titans matchup? All of that open field and Troy went mano a mano with the 4.2 40-yard dash champ in Johnson, and won. Troy bagged him like a hungry wolf taking down its prey. On the next series, well deep on the other side of the 50-yard line, he defended the aforementioned bomb to

Britt. It was an incredible show of athleticism early in a game in which an injury curtailed the rest of what had been a most promising season.

Along with that superhuman athleticism, Troy was a calculated risk-taker. He possessed an absolutely fearless attitude. I don't know of anyone, short of Evel Knievel, who rolled the dice the way Polamalu did. If you download a Polamalu highlights video, watch how he Superman'ed Collins and Joe Flacco on quarterback sneaks, or ran through the A gap against the Bengals to take down Andy Dalton after beating the pants off two big shaggies. Troy had *Dancing with the Stars*–level timing. He was seemingly guided by an innate inner rhythm that only he could tune in to. And in big moments, he tuned in and took those risks. And let's face it, once you're airborne on a QB sneak, there's no going back.

So take that athleticism, mix in an abundance of courage, and then add the towering intellect that came from oversaturating his game prep in the film-study room, and you had Troy's incredible ability to disguise coverage. What's more, the way he disguised his intentions was paramount to his success. He could "sugar up" a coverage scheme like Martha Stewart making Christmas cookies. Meaning, loads of sugar, everywhere.

His teammates used to laugh while they told stories of Troy, how he would "coffeehouse" and hang in the nether world of secondary depth, moving back and forth so that his intentions were baffling to a quarterback trying to get a pre-snap read. Troy could seemingly Jedi a quarterback and suck in his thoughts like a tractor beam. He could read a quarterback's eyes and mind better than a *CSI* profiler.

Was he not renting space in Flacco's head? While quarterbacking the Ravens, Flacco said simply that his pre-snap read was to "follow the hair." In 2010, when the Steelers were playing in Baltimore, the game was on the line and the Ravens were driving. Troy coffeehoused by lining up around linebacker depth. He waited for Flacco—who was looking over the defense—to turn his head. When Flacco looked away, Polamalu sunk down to the end of the line of scrimmage next to James Harrison.

At the snap, Polamalu blitzed and creamed Flacco from the blind side. The ball came loose and LaMarr Woodley recovered. The Steelers went on to win the game, the division, then the conference, and of course Super Bowl XLIII in Tampa.

Troy was just one of those guys whom the ball always seemed to find, though of course it was the other way around. Some guys have that skill, luck, or good fortune, but most don't. Looking over his stellar career—including 32 interceptions, 14 forced fumbles, and 7 fumble recoveries—you become acutely aware that Troy had that knack for finding the ball. Ricochets, bounces, timely strips, and sacks were always a part of his production. How many times did we see him pull in an overthrow that caromed off the hands of a receiver? Or witness a fumbled ball that just laid on the ground and nobody seemed to notice but Troy? In the act of taking down an opponent, Troy had the knack of stripping the ball when it was just inches off the ground. Remember the game in Green Bay when the great Brett Favre was strip-sacked? Troy picked it up and cruised to a touchdown while watching the Jumbotron to see if anybody was catching up to him.

Troy's list of superlatives is stunningly superlative, but to me, the essence of his greatness, and what separated him from so many other players, was his ability to see the play instinctually. He was playing three-dimensional chess while the other guys were playing checkers. I often reference the samurai sixth sense. I truly believe in this. In martial arts terminology, if you asked an old *karateka*, he would tell you it's called *mushin*, meaning mind/no mind. Some players describe it as the game slowing down, or being in the zone. But I think it's more than just turning off the chatter in your head. It's a disciplined approach to performing a task or skill, the result of years of preparation and perseverance. It's moving beyond just the physical aspect of the game in order to combine one's great attributes with the instinctual, and then being willing to trust and act on those instincts. It's rarified air for those who are able to attain the mental ability and clarity to do this. And some "just do" much better than others.

I watched Troy over his career. After a series on the field, he would head back to the bench. There would be some interaction and chatter with other teammates and coaches, to be sure, but at some point he would withdraw into himself. At times, to an outside observer, he appeared to be unaware of his surroundings and what was happening on the field. But I believe he was more tuned in than anybody else. I believe his greatest attribute was his ability to lock in to the rhythm of the game, set aside all distraction, enter *mushin*, slow the game down, and focus like a laser beam on the task at hand.

Think I'm kidding? Read his own words: "I think there comes a point in the game where you're not cognitively thinking, you just kind of see where everything develops, the way the offensive linemen come up, the way they get set. You kind of see their splits. You kind of see the quarterback's energy. And the more and more you play the game of football, the more and more you have a sensitivity to the rhythm of the football game."

That's the voice of a Hall of Famer, a player who changed the way his position would be played, the same way Lawrence Taylor changed the game in his era. If you still don't understand, break out your *Karate Kid* videotape and give a listen to Mr. Miyagi. "Wax on, wax off."

CHAPTER 24

DAWG POUND DAYS

"Heads up!" someone in the huddle suddenly yelped. It threw those of us bunched closely together in the end zone into a state of instant readiness. We suddenly formed the phalanx battle formation out of ancient Sparta. Normally, hanging out in the huddle during the two-minute warning, waiting to assume victory formation, is a simple matter. After the ref whistles in the clock, it's snap the ball, take the knee, and wait for time to expire. It's a perfunctory, matter-of-fact end-of-game sequence of events that caps off a great day and allows for a satisfied smile. Taking a knee in a visiting, hostile environment was even better; it added to the smugness of the moment we were feeling.

We had fought hard all day. We put up more points on the board than our opponent, and a couple of kneeldowns and a quick bus trip back to the 'Burgh were awaiting us. A win at home is always the best, but a win on the road has a special taste of satisfaction and flavor that is difficult to convey unless you've been there, done that. And it *never* gets old doing so in Cleveland.

Playing in Cleveland required a certain level of readiness that was different from other NFL stadiums, especially in the end zone, where the infamous Dawg Pound was located. It carried with it league-wide infamy, and that's the correct word choice. The Dawg Pound housed the slightly skewed, feverish, and potentially aggressive Cleveland Browns fans. They congregated there and cheered, crudely gestured, yelled obscenities, and threw things. They were a dog-mask-wearing, biscuit-throwing, crazy train of Browns backers who pressed the very limits of fandom. It got so bad over the years that security cameras were installed in that end zone to identify any armchair warriors who took their cheering a little too seriously. To put that in perspective, this was well before security cameras became the norm post-9/11.

An object whizzed by our heads as we looked up and narrowly missed being hit by a full beer can. It landed near me, right around the 2-yard line. Over the years I'd seen batteries, dog bones, all sorts of things. But an unopened adult beverage? This was a first. Some seriously misguided Browns fan was apparently very unhappy with us. Feeling a little thirsty, not to mention a little antagonistic toward the crowd, I eyeballed the can, turned to Mike Webster, and said, "I'm thinking about going over there, picking that can up, popping the top, and saluting the crowd. Whaddaya think?"

Mike laughed, then turned a little more serious as he saw the look on my face. "If you do that, just know that you will start a riot such as never been seen before in the history of the NFL. The ref may cancel the game, and Chuck will make you walk home in your uniform and cleats before cutting you." I mulled it over. As tantalizing as the thought of a sip and salute to the crowd might be, the thought of walking home in spikes closed the deal.

The Cleveland Browns. The Turnpike Rivalry. I'd heard about it before I experienced it. The veterans of the '70s, before my time, told stories of playing in Cleveland with its rowdy crowds and driving back and forth on the Pennsylvania/Ohio Turnpike. I'd heard the stories of cars with Pennsylvania plates being vandalized in the parking lots in Cleveland, among many other sordid misdeeds committed by fans. Teammates of mine who were veterans of playing in Cleveland and had family members who'd had uncomfortable experiences in Cleveland warned the rookies about having their family travel to Cleveland. I'm not joking—when we played there, my family would literally drive to a cousin's house on the east side of Cleveland, park the car, and then ride to the stadium with the cousin in his Ohio-plated car. And they only did that once or twice because the fans were too aggressive!

Cleveland Municipal Stadium was both massive and poorly designed. There were seats located behind gigantic support beams running vertically from the lower bowl that supported the upper deck. Built in the early 1930s next to the city's harbor, the aging stadium justly earned its nickname the Mistake on the Lake. Even worse, the stadium housed

There was nothing like playing at the Cleveland Dawg Pound in the early '80s.
Courtesy of the Pittsburgh Steelers

lousy locker-room facilities that had been built for baseball teams. Too few lockers meant doubling and tripling up with teammates. Three guys to a locker meant having to dress in shifts, and of course the veterans always dressed first. You knew you had attained official veteran status in the eyes of legendary Steelers equipment man Tony Parisi when you got your own locker in Cleveland. A tunnel from the locker room that led to the baseball dugout, from which you would emerge onto the playing field, smelled of urine. (Apparently, baseball players chose to relieve themselves in the tunnel instead of going all the way back up to the locker room.) And though I had been warned, I never could have prepared for the intensity, ferocity, and bloodletting howl that seemed to accompany every Steelers/Browns clash. The games were savagely played and bitterly fought, both on the field and in the stands.

I remember Jack Lambert in the middle of a melee on the Browns' side of the field, and an embittered Chuck Noll in a postgame press conference describing how Jack had been "kicked where a young man shouldn't be kicked." The fights that flared up spontaneously on the playing field were too numerous to list. Such was the rivalry that existed between us back in the 1980s. Simply put, these were two teams with great legacies from hardcore football towns. And the fans who followed these teams from Rust Belt steel towns that had suffered severe economic hardship through the downturn of the steel industry were just as tough. Football bragging rights are serious business along this corridor.

Indoctrination came as early as my first trip to Cleveland. It was during pregame in a stadium that housed nearly 80,000 fans when, while warming up near the infamous Dawg Pound, Steelers all-time great defensive end Dwight White reprimanded both Tunch Ilkin and me for unbuckling our helmets and taking them off. "No, no, no, young bucks!" Mad Dog said in a stern voice that was loud enough to overcome the fans "barking" in the stands. "Don't *ever* take your helmets off in the Dawg Pound."

Dog biscuits normally greeted us when we hit the field in Cleveland, since we had to warm up in the end zone in front of the Dawg Pound. The wall that separated the fans from the players was low, nearly ground level and *very* close to the back of the end zone. The nearby lunacy of the venom spewing from the fans took me by surprise. I had never experienced such out-and-out hatred. The incredible amount of booing and vitriol that rolled in from the upper levels, pouring down over the cavernous lower stands and out onto the field, was nothing I had ever encountered either.

I played in Cleveland at least a dozen times, and I can tell you that I only remember one—count 'em, one—sunny day out of all those games. So perhaps it's no surprise that this is a town whose river famously caught on fire. The one sunny day in Cleveland that I remember was on a Sunday. The field was muddy after Pink Floyd had played a concert there two days earlier. Apparently the Pink Floyd fans had gotten a little rowdy too. They had torn up the turf so much that the grounds crew was forced to procure sand from the shore of nearby Lake Erie to fill in the divots. Worse, the sand smelled of dead fish. I'm not kidding—dead, rotten, smelly fish! Suffice it to say, the conditions were not ideal. During the game, while in the midst of stuffing a bull rush from Clay Matthews, I stepped into a sandy, fishy hole that nearly blew out my knee.

Part of the intensity of the fierce rivalry stemmed from the fact that our coach, Chuck Noll, was born in Cleveland and played for the Browns before he went to Pittsburgh. Whenever it was Cleveland week, there was a noticeable rise in intensity emanating from Coach. Not that he wasn't always intense, mind you, but Coach Noll's Browns Week practices inevitably became longer, with more reps in all the team periods. Apparently we were getting ready for any and every possible football circumstance, from the single wing to any slight variation of any standard football formation and play that could be contemplated. Every play was run until Coach was satisfied, even if it had to be run several times. Chuck simply refused to be outcoached, even if it meant outcoaching himself.

In my rookie year, we beat the Browns at Three Rivers Stadium. I was playing left guard in the short-yardage and goal-line packages then. In the final seconds of the game, we had a first-and-goal at the 2- or 3-yard line. We needed a touchdown to win. Believe it or not, we ran the same play—sprint right pick—three times in a row because Coach Noll believed the play would and should work. And by golly, it was going to work—even if he had to lose the game to prove it!

Of course, the Browns knew the play was coming by the second attempt, and they were calling it out when we came to the line of scrimmage. Terry Bradshaw had even tried to talk Chuck out of running it again during a timeout before third down. But Coach wouldn't listen. Bradshaw threw the game-winner to Lynn Swann (and yes, there was an illegal pick involved) with 11 seconds left in the game.

Coach Noll refused to listen to other voices when he was convinced of his own, and it was one of the many reasons he was so successful. Coach always reminded us that "Practice doesn't make perfect; *perfect* practice makes perfect"—even if you had to practice something over and over to achieve the sought-after perfection.

One Browns Week practice, during a Friday before a Sunday game, we were running short-yardage and goal-line plays—in full pads and full contact, per usual. We ran Toss 28 U crack back, which featured Tunch Ilkin pulling from his right tackle position and leading the running back out on the perimeter to block on an outside running play. We ran it over and over, seeking a perfection that was missing in Coach Noll's eyes. And I mean to tell you, we ran it 17 times in a row! You read that right. I checked with our offensive coordinator, Tom Moore, a few years ago when I saw him. He had a chuckle over the memory.

As a matter of fact, after another week of high-volume, ballistic practices in another year, I recall jogging from the dugout in Cleveland. I was feeling exhausted before we even began warm-ups. As we jogged down toward the Dawg Pound, I turned to Tunch and said sarcastically, "Have you seen my legs? They were here a couple days ago, but I can't feel them now." They literally felt as stiff as boards. And I wasn't alone in feeling worn out after a hard week of prep for Cleveland.

But of course, the searing intensity didn't just happen in Cleveland. The Browns coming to Three Rivers was tantamount to a playoff game in Pittsburgh. Our fans were waiting, and their fevered pitch was demonstrable by their actions in the stands. I remember once, after the Browns beat us at Three Rivers Stadium in 1986 to end our 16-game winning streak against them there. Ozzie Newsome, the great TE for the Browns, walked slowly as he looked around the stadium while Tunch and I shook hands with him. At one point, he quizzically looked past us and said, "I want to enjoy this. I've never won a game here in Pittsburgh."

And I know all of Steelers Nation is still smarting from that loss to the Browns in the 2020 playoffs. But at least the Steelers came back to make a game of it. When the Browns beat us 51–0 at Three Rivers Stadium to open the 1989 season, the game was totally out of hand—the worst loss in Steelers history. The Browns defense forced eight turnovers and sacked Bubby Brister six times. It felt like there was a turnover going the other way every time we had the ball. Tim Worley lost three fumbles, including two in a 17-point Browns first quarter in which their defense created all of the scoring. The Browns led 30–0 at halftime. I mean, they dominated us and led by an unbelievable 19 to 5 in first downs and 357 to 53 in total yards. We crossed midfield only once in the first half. *Ouch.*

Getting off the field after a Browns game was always important. Malingering was never a good idea. And in my day, NFL field-level security wasn't where it is now. In 1986, at Cleveland, we played into sudden-death overtime. When we saw our cornerback, covering Webster Slaughter on an out-and-up route, fall down on the muddy field and Cleveland QB Bernie Kosar launch a perfect strike, we headed for the locker room almost before Slaughter caught the ball.

Whenever we played in Cleveland, there always seemed to be something out of the ordinary that happened. Once Randy Grossman missed the team buses to Cleveland and took his own car. He raced ahead of the buses and beat us there. Then there was the time when, the night before a game at the team hotel, a drunken Browns fan opened the door to the room where Tunch Ilkin and I were sacked out. It was the middle of the night. I slept through the whole thing, but an irate Tunch ushered the man on his way. Apparently, whoever had done the bed check that night had left the door slightly ajar.

During a preseason game we played in Cleveland back in 1981, Tunch was playing center, his college position, and I was at left guard. Cliff Stoudt was the QB. Tunch had been battling an intestinal issue throughout training camp and he would, at some point, have such an overabundance of acid percolating in his gullet that he would vomit. And when he did, it was intense. The team doctors diagnosed it as projectile vomitus. (Nice, huh?)

In the second half of that game, I entered for Sam Davis and Tunch was in for Mike Webster. In the huddle, a 3 trap was called. While we were at the line of scrimmage and the QB was calling out the snap count, I heard Tunch gurgling, trying to hold it in. Tunch and I had been assigned to double-team the Browns' nose tackle. Perfectly timed, and synchronized with the snap of the ball, Tunch vomited straight in the face of the NT, who was merely inches away from Tunch's face mask. Such was the timing that the guy, so shocked and blinded by the fire hose of Gatorade and pregame meal, he stood straight up trying to get it off his face. We double-teamed the poor guy about 10 yards off the ball. Stoudt found it so humorous that in the huddle, after seeing how well the play turned out, he asked Tunch, "Got anything left? Let's run that play again!"

The Browns came up with a new wrinkle the next year on defense when they had their nose tackle playing a soft zero technique. Instead of crowding the line of scrimmage, he lined up a yard or so off the ball. Rumor had it that Tunch was the inspiration.

Those were the days. And Cleveland was quite the place.

CHAPTER 25

STAGE FRIGHT

"Did you sing yet?"

The question itself was easy enough. I mean, you either sang or you didn't. Not much wiggle room there. I mean, it wasn't like one of Chuck Noll's infamous trick questions. But there was a bigger problem: I was terrified of singing in public.

I come from a long line of notable wailers. And by that I mean stone-cold, tone-deaf family members who couldn't carry a tune with a wheelbarrow. My grandfather Ed Palmer, a simply wonderful man—a God-loving, God-fearing man—sang so badly in church that people unfamiliar with his tone-deafness would look at him with alarm during the singing of a hymn. They might have thought he was in the midst of a medical event. Seriously. One friend of mine called Grandpa Palmer's singing voice "akin to that of a braying mule." Come on, that's about as tone-deaf as it gets.

So there I was, in the cafeteria at St. Vincent College during my rookie year in 1980. The old tradition of rookies singing at camp was in full bloom when I came to the team (nowadays, for all intents and purposes, it's long gone). I had spent a full week and a half, during two-a-days, hustling off the field and getting in and out of lunch and dinner as quickly as possible. Get in, stuff my face, and slide back out through the rear of the cafeteria hoping that the slower-moving, older, established veterans wouldn't see me. Of course, there was usually some extra time available because some of the vets would head out before dinner to "replenish their fluids," per Coach Noll's advice, at a veteran-approved watering hole.

On this particular evening, I had been a little slow getting off the practice field. I was tired, beat up, and moving slowly—which put me right in the middle of the dinner crowd. At this point I should say that for those of you who pooh-pooh the trauma of getting up in front of 150 or so of your peers—which in my case included players, coaches, trainers, owners, media, and then those among the cafeteria staff—well, then you

Rookies who sing together stay together. Tunch Ilkin (left) and I were lifelong friends. Courtesy of the Pittsburgh Steelers

sing better than me. All I can tell you is that I avoided the dinner crowd like the plague.

Sure, I bet none of you would mind being called out in front of everybody to stand on a suspiciously wobbly chair and attempt to gain everybody's attention and quiet the room. Then, when all eyes are on you, you'll announce your name, your hometown, and what school you attended. Go on, introduce the number with which you are going to entertain that evening's dinner crowd. All in a voice that had better be booming. Timidity only gets you more repetitions. Oh, and don't forget your microphone. Unless you were crooning into your mic—a soup spoon borrowed from the St. Vincent cutlery collection—the veterans would claim they couldn't hear you and make you start over.

And that's when the insults start. If it was a rowdy day on the field, the jeers might become more personal. If it was just a regular practice, the dinner crowd might be a little more tolerant. Either way, you aren't going to come out of the song unscathed, unless of course you homer it. In all my 12 years of professional football, including 11 professionally harassing amateur crooners in the dining hall, I believe there were only a couple drop-the-mic, walk-off moments.

The rowdiest receptions always occurred during dinner. Few were the lunch singers. I mean, it's hard to be jovial when you're facing the second of two two-and-a-half-hour practices each day in 90-degree heat and humidity. Humor came in short supply in the afternoon. Guys just wanted to get back to the dorms and take a nap after the morning practice. So that's why the evening times were so much better. And coarser.

At the evening meal, two-a-days were in the barn. All that remained on the day's docket was the infernal two-and-a-half-hour evening meeting.

"Did you sing yet?" Though the question of performing was daunting enough, the real fear trickling through me on this day was because of the person asking. Joe Greene. Check that—"Mean" Joe Greene. The greatest slayer of offensive lines in the history of the NFL.

What do you do? Do you just stand up for yourself and say, "No, it ain't gonna happen"? Do you try your luck and lie? Or do you just grudgingly acquiesce and get up on the wobbly chair and have at it?

I was in a pickle for sure. A sudden attack of raspy dryness caused my tongue to become instantly dysfunctional. The terror of singing in front of Chuck Noll, Mr. Rooney, the ever-scowling Jack Lambert, Mike Webster, Terry Bradshaw, and the great mocker of rookies Dwight "Mad Dog" White. To endure the derisive, booming laughter of L. C. Greenwood and the plastic cups, confetti, or whatever other detritus thrown by the always amiable Steve Furness was, well, terrifying. But no. This was no place for shrinking violets. Simon Cowell couldn't hold a candle to the hostile commentary that this crowd at St. Vincent College held in store. As a matter of fact, Simon probably would've gotten himself beat up by this bunch.

I found myself tractor-beamed into Joe's intense gaze, and all thoughts of lying quickly dissipated. I'm not sure exactly what I said, but if heaven has a transcript of my reply, I believe it was along the lines of, "Ummm, no, I, uh, h-haven't singed—er, I mean snug—hmmm, sunged—uh, yet."

The part I definitively remember with absolute clarity is Joe's eyebrows. They rose slightly and showed a touch of amusement over my sudden attack of stupidity and inability to string a couple sentences together.

"Do you want to sing?" Oh, this had to be the trick question of all trick questions! Do I *want* to sing? Are you kidding me? Was Joe Greene about to show mercy to a rookie? Before I could stutter and stumble through another answer, Joe leaned forward and jerked his thumb toward the stage and said, "Go sing." There was no bargaining room available in the tone of his voice. The look in his eyes backed up that voice.

I numbly rose from my seat and felt all the blood in my body rush to my face. I had been trying to avoid this throughout the first couple weeks of camp. It was as if I had just knocked down a shot of cold medicine and everything seemed to suddenly slow down to a crawl. I began the slow trek toward the "stage," and that's when the sudden inspiration hit me like a bolt of lightning. I saw my fellow rookie offensive lineman Tunch Ilkin sitting in his chair on the aisle, looking at me as if I was headed to my doom. In a quick, desperate attempt to make it a duet rather than a solo, I leaned over and told Tunch that Joe wanted us to sing. Tunch immediately looked back at Joe, who, unaware of what I had said, just kept staring and nodding, as if that idea had come straight from his lips. Tunch, of course, got to his feet and started to follow me, no idea that he had just been bamboozled.

We huddled for a moment when we reached the stage. In an increasing panic, and due to the restlessness of the dinner crowd, we settled on the only song both of us knew: the tune from the old Western show *Rawhide*.

Once the chairs of the stage had been assembled and we were handed our "microphones," Tunch kicked off the number. But we had to start over again because we had forgotten our proper introductions.

"Rolling, rolling, rolling! Keep them doggies rolling, RAWHIDE!" Oh, we went after it hard—loud and boisterous, complete with a couple air whips cracking the imaginary cattle. Of course our timing was completely off. Then after stumbling our way through the first verse, I forgot the words to the second verse. So naturally I continued with a second run of the first verse, which completely threw Tunch off. From there it began melting down into an incomprehensible muddle of cracking the whip, mumbling "keep them doggies rolling," followed by the inevitable, intermittent, out-of-place punctuation of "RAWHIDE!" which I kept yelling awkwardly, as if I was being shocked with a cattle prod.

Well, you can only imagine the laughter, which then became intermixed with disbelief over how lousy our torturous rendition of "Rawhide" was unfolding. The serious booing started from the back of the room and made its way forward like a wave to the shore. It then ran into the low smattering of boos emanating from the front rows. The convergence of the two waves caused the din to grow louder until finally the cascade of boos reached tsunami status. Everybody—and I do mean everybody, including the kitchen staff—had a boo going. We were mercifully kicked offstage before we got around to verse three.

I can't even begin to tell you the number of hecklers—from the equipment guys to the trainers and of course the coaches and players—who razzed us for the rest of camp. But there was solace in one thing: We were so bad that nobody even dared suggest a second engagement. Hall and Oates, Seals and Crofts, Loggins and Messina, sure. But Wolfley and Ilkin? Not so much.

There is a postscript to this story. Once it became known that Tunch technically had volunteered to sing, he was called out to go solo a week or so later. He stirred the hearts of everyone with a curious rendition of "Love Potion No. 9." And though I can't remember the exact circumstances that allowed me to sit in my chair while Tunch went solo, I certainly didn't mind.

I didn't boo. But boy, did I laugh!

CHAPTER 26

THE BIG CRAMP

Players are at the mercy of NFL schedule-makers. The guys in the backrooms, boardrooms, and the rest of the what-have-you-rooms of the NFL executive offices on Park Avenue in the Big Apple have all the formulas from one year to the next. Who's gonna play whom? When? Where? Those sorts of things.

It's always an interesting moment when the schedule is released. The secret recipe is well above my pay grade, but as a player in the league for 12 years, I always found it useful to take a few quiet moments to peruse the season in the big picture in order to highlight certain aspects.

For instance, playing the Jerry Glanville–coached Houston Oilers in the latter part of the 1980s took on a whole new meaning compared to the bums of the Bum Phillips era. Cheap shots, including vicious blind-side hits meant to inflict injury, were as normal as Glanville leaving game tickets for Elvis. Playing in Seattle was always a long, tiring, grueling trip. The Kingdome, where the Seahawks used to play, always seemed to morph into a *Twilight Zone* episode, complete with Rod Serling wearing a striped shirt and whistle. A home game in Three Rivers Stadium against the Cleveland Browns was, for all intents and purposes, a guaranteed win—at least for the first half of the '80s. Then it flipped the other way and we couldn't get a dubya against the Browns on our home turf to save our lives. Strong teams become weak teams, losers become winners; such are the nuances of NFL life that ebb and flow, constantly altering the landscape.

But there was always a certainty that you never wanted to bump up against, especially if you had a proclivity for cramping. And that was playing a team in the South in December for us guys coming in from the Northeast. I was forever on alert for games in which you could encounter wild swings in temperatures—times when we'd practice at home in 20-degree weather then board a flight for a so-called wonderful, palm-tree-laden paradise. Sure, it's nice to get out of bad weather and see the sun, but you can bet it's going to be uncomfortable. For a football player, an 80- or 90-degree day in Miami is wonderful in late February and March but never in late November or December.

Flying into any NFL city for a game is no day at the beach, to be sure. There's work to be done, and acquiring and maintaining proper focus requires sacrifice and a good dose of determination. Margaritaville is no place to get your mind straight before an NFL game. I know the greyhounds—the pass-catching extraordinaires such as Lynn Swann, John Stallworth, and Louis Lipps—loved this kind of weather. (Coincidentally, those guys hailed from San Mateo, California; Tuscaloosa, Alabama; and New Orleans, Louisiana. I don't see any Buffalo, New York, on the list.)

Hey, what can I say? I'm of Northeastern descent. My people hail from four-season climates. The blood coursing through my veins is more akin to 10W motor oil perpetually winterizing my innards. Subtropical weather is as anathema to me as rain to the Tin Man. Put me out in short sleeves with a T-shirt underneath my shoulder pads and I'm good to go, baby. Below-zero wind chill temps and blizzard conditions never bothered me. We fat guys can run all day in weather like that. As far as I'm concerned, adrenaline is a wonderful warmer-upper.

On the other hand, when the heat and humidity creep up toward clambake temperatures, I've experienced multiple misadventures in hydration. Practice or game, it's always the same. Understand now, I never fell out. I always finished. The Big Cramp was polite, always seeming to wait to set in until after the game or practice was over. The boil out would begin back in the locker room. It was like I just couldn't seem to slow down or shut off the internal air-conditioning unit that God gave me. I'd be sweating buckets of sweat, pulling off the pads, and stripping down to shorts, trying to will my body to cool down. But my inner thermostat seemed forever stuck on high. Gatorade, salts, special formulas...nothing staved off the inevitable. And when the cramps started to set in, I knew it wasn't going to end well for me.

Coming through camp and then playing warm-weather games was one thing. That, I could handle for the most part because the swing wasn't extreme. Inevitably I would start to cramp, but that would cause me to make sure that I was rehydrating properly, and then I was good to go. But early on as a young buck, not knowing that I was in particular need of extra hydration, I suffered through those blasted muscle cramps. But then once I got through the hot and humid part of the season—say, on into November or December—I could relax. But if that schedule showed a warm-weather game in a far-off, distant land, it was always a red flag.

Remember, back in my day teams always practiced outside. There weren't any indoor practice barns, much less the kind that could be heated to simulate a warm-weather game, such as there are today. But that's what you really need to prepare for warm weather. It helps your body regulate the huge loss of fluids. Practicing in cold weather simply can't do it. So when I noticed a game in Miami on the schedule, it was always, "Danger, Will Robinson. Danger!"

One frosty winter day in Pittsburgh we took off and landed in warm and muggy Miami. The game-day forecast was bright and sunny for the 1:00 kickoff. The temperature was in the 80s, along with a good dose of humidity to ensure it was going to be miserable in the trenches. It was so hot and sunny, legendary center Mike Webster eschewed his thigh, knee, and hip pads; "the lighter the load the better," Webbie said.

Kickoff came and went. Halftime came and went. The sweltering Miami sun began taking its toll as we got deeper into the second half. Breathing huge gulps of air after a long drive felt like sucking the exhaust pipe of a car. On our first offensive drive in the third quarter, we ran the most basic staple of our trapping offense. I could run this play in my sleep: Toss 32 trap. From split backs, I would pull from left guard and trap the area over right guard/right tackle. Tunch Ilkin, the right tackle, would pass set and club his man to the outside. Terry Long, playing right guard, would double-team with Webster on the Miami nose tackle and then get the backside, inside linebacker.

I pulled from left guard, turned up in the hole, and powerfully clashed with inside linebacker John Offerdahl, a superb 3-4 inside linebacker. John knew how to play the inside trap. As soon as he saw Long step inside on a double-team block with Webster, Offerdahl sparked and got his downhill bang on. After the initial collision, as I was trying to dig him out of the hole, which incidentally felt like pushing a small car up a hill, I felt my right quad cramp. It quickly released after a momentary spasm, just enough to let me know trouble was on the way. *Oh boy...in the first series of the second half? Yikes.*

The game continued, and though I gave my best effort guzzling Gatorade, water, and anything else the trainers had, I was still feeling intermittent tweaks, twinges, and pops. I knew I was in for cramping after the game—that much was obvious. What's more, you can't swill liquids without paying a price for it. You can't move with catlike stealth and quickness when you're bloated like a beach ball.

We came to the bench after another failed drive in the third quarter, me gulping Gatorade and water like it was going out of style. One of our offensive line coaches approached while we were catching our breath and we went over some problematic game situations and made sure we were all on the same page. Long, a terrific guard from East Carolina University and an extremely strong dude, was breathing like a locomotive after an uphill climb. He just couldn't slow his breathing down. So our offensive line coach turned to Terry and asked, "Do you need a break?" Terry, drawing a huge draft of furnace-quality air, spit out, "Put the kid in," referring to rookie Brian Blankenship from Nebraska. That singular directive from Terry became one of those legendary quotes that would reverberate in hysterics whenever the story of Terry Long and the Miami Dolphins came up over the years. We all got a good laugh over that. Never one to laugh at himself too easily, even Terry chuckled about it...years later.

Playing against the Dolphins in the Miami heat was never easy, even when you're double-teaming with the great Mike Webster (52).
Courtesy of the Pittsburgh Steelers

The game ended and we lost. I went out to shake hands with some of the guys, say hi to Danny Marino, and head off toward the players tunnel, all while trying to be careful not to flex anything too forcefully. Once I got to the locker room, I sat down on the stool at my locker and began pulling off the pads and cutting the tape off my hands, ankles, and finally my knee. I could feel the muscles begin to twinge, tweak, and spasm with a little more urgency. Let me tell you—it's such a weird feeling. Calmly, I tried to drink more water, but I already felt as if my gullet was going to split from all the liquids I had forced down. I was semi-hopeful I might actually stave off the cramps and get myself into the shower and sit under a cold spigot. If I could just do that, then maybe, just maybe, the blasted cramps would stay away.

All I knew for sure was that if the trainers thought I was going to lock up, they wouldn't let me on the bus from Joe Robbie Stadium to the airport. And if they wouldn't let me on the bus, I was not going to get on the plane. And if I didn't get on the team plane, well, that meant it was off to the hospital. And that meant I'd have to stay overnight in Miami and travel on my own back to Pittsburgh the next day, my only day off.

As I was mulling all of this over, I guess it became fairly obvious to our head trainer, Ralph "the Plumber" Berlin what was going on, and then it started with a bang. Oh, geez, Louise, did it start! I was sitting on the stool in front of my locker, trying to lie and fake my way out of the muscles locking up in an effort to get on that bus before the locker room totally emptied out. Calves, quads, and then hammies all seized up. I started to look like a marionette puppet with someone jerking my strings. Teammates sitting near me were giving me that sympathetic have-fun-at-the-hospital look as the intensity of my cramps increased.

I began pleading with Ralph to give me more time, assuring him that the cramps would fade and I would be all right. *Just a little more time, man, please, I don't want to go to the hospital.*

More cramps. But now my low back and chest muscles joined in. At this point, Tunch was sitting on the bus. He overheard several of the guys on the bus betting whether I was going to make it or lock up. Apparently it was even money at that point.

Until the ambulance showed up outside the locker room. "He ain't going to make it," Tunch announced.

Grudgingly I accepted the inevitable and allowed myself to get on the stretcher. With a solemn face, I came to grips with my fate, knowing that all the boys were sitting outside in the air-conditioned buses and I would be wheeled out in front of them. As they began to stuff me in the back of the ambulance, I heard the buses honk and the gears grind as they began to leave. Man, I didn't even look at them. I just wanted to go home. But they were leaving me.

At least the only ambulance trip of my life was a *little* interesting. The two attending EMTs were Cuban-born, loved calypso music, hated Castro, and were jamming as we made our way to the hospital. They were pretty funny guys, actually. They kept the entertainment factor up as my dauber was going down. I was driven to Key Biscayne Hospital. Don't remember much about my stay other than the Dolphins' team doctor, Edward St. Mary, came by to see me. I was plugged with several bags of saline solution, got some late-afternoon rest from the heat in the excellent hospital air-conditioning, and settled in for the night. He was an excellent doctor, and he made sure that I had a large pizza and some adult beverages delivered to my room after I was unplugged from the IV bags. Okay, so it wasn't a bad way to end the day. All things considered, though, I'd rather have been back in the 'Burgh.

The next day I had to wait to be discharged, go through the usual physical before I could check out, and then fly to Atlanta to catch a flight to Pittsburgh. Suffice it to say, traveling on the team plane is so much better. Finally, the doctor on call at the hospital came in. He was a smaller man, and he peered at me through large, black-rimmed glasses. I couldn't read his name tag, so I began to think of him as Doctor Spectacles.

"I see you cramped up yesterday," said the good doc as he peered at me and the chart loaded with papers in front of him. "It was very warm yesterday. Were you outside a lot?" I'm guessing he was not a football fan.

"Yes, I was outside all afternoon, Doc," I replied with a laugh, thinking he was goofing on me. Surely he knew what I had been doing, right?

"Were you doing yard work?" he asked.

Hmm? Seriously? Now I figured he had to be messing with me, so I played along. "Uh-huh. It was a really big yard, Doc, a really big yard."

"I hope you weren't using a push mower."

"Afraid so, Doc, I was pushing all day long."

"Did you feel these cramps coming on as you were doing the yard work?"

"Uh-huh."

"Did you tell anybody or take a break?"

"Nope. Had to get the job done, Doc."

Doctor Spectacles wrote ambitiously on his clipboard for a little while, peering at me occasionally and tsk-tsking me with little shakes of his head. I was coming to the conclusion that the dear doc was not aware of my occupation or circumstances that had plopped me into his hospital on this fine, full-of-sunshine Miami Monday morning.

"Well, we are going to release you, Mr. Wolfley. I hope this is a lesson to you that though you are young and strong, you need to stay hydrated and be careful, especially in hot weather. Good day."

Good day, Doc. Good day off.

CHAPTER 27

GENTLENESS AND STRENGTH

The world lost a shining star when God brought a modern-day Samson, Don Reinhoudt, home into His kingdom on July 3, 2023. He will forever be remembered for his strength and kindness, the inspiration he sparked everywhere, and the love and memories he left us. He was truly one of the most amazing men I've ever known.

Don Reinhoudt of Brocton, New York, was widely acknowledged throughout the '70s and '80s as the World's Strongest Man. He became the first International Powerlifting Federation Superheavyweight World Champion, a title he won in four consecutive years. The man simultaneously held the squat, bench press, deadlift, and total records in the superheavyweight class and won the coveted World's Strongest Man title in 1979. He was also one of the best men God ever created.

Don was a living legend who hailed from my part of the country. A man with a heart bigger than even his massive 6'4", 365-pound body should've allowed, Reinhoudt had 23-inch biceps and a 62-inch chest. His forearms measured 18½ inches. I'm telling you, I wouldn't have believed any of it if I hadn't seen it.

Growing up in Orchard Park, one couldn't help but hear of his exploits. His hometown, Brocton, was just down the thruway from my home, probably an hour or so away. And I read anything I could about him. As a growing teenager and offensive lineman in the making, I avidly sought to become stronger. I began weight lifting in earnest over at my buddies' house. Brian, Gary, and Mike were brothers, and best friends with me and my two younger brothers, Dale and Ron. We met through church and quickly became inseparable. Oh, did we ever have fun!

Weight lifting was a bond that really brought us together. A lot of great lifting can get done with just the basics: a bar, lots of weights, a bench, and a willingness to train hard. I was dedicated to reaching the next level in my lifting. In my unquenchable desire to learn, I was always seeking out new information and asking questions. After all, I was on a quest to get to the NFL; getting stronger was a necessary part of that quest.

I never shied away from competition. Good or bad, I was never afraid to get in the ring and test myself, whether it was football, boxing, powerlifting, or strongman competitions. I once even competed in a quasi-professional tug-of-war contest! If you really want to know dirt-tired, enter one of those. Guys dig in on a sandy beach like a tick on a hound, six to eight men a team. It's seriously one of the most grueling contests I ever endured. It'll fry your forearms, to be sure, *and* it will test your will.

But the powerlifts—the bench, squat, deadlift—were the basic power builders of my day. We didn't have fancy training facilities, or speed and power camps, as young players do today. It was basic strength training in its most raw and elemental form. After a few years of intense training on the three powerlifts, naturally it was time to test myself and see how I stacked up against competition. Well, Nashua, New Hampshire, was the site of the Teenage National Powerlifting Championships. This was in the late '70s. I qualified to compete and was pretty excited to go. My mom and dad traveled with me, and I ended up doing well there. But what changed the course of my life was that Don Reinhoudt was there.

Don had just won his fourth world title the previous year and was in the process of dropping weight from the superheavyweight class (360–370 pounds) to the newly formed 275-pound class. Believe me, he was still impressively huge, and I was in awe. Don was there with his wife, Cindy, helping another young man who had trained with him. I struck up a conversation with Don and asked the usual neophyte questions, things a world champion might expect. He was friendly, patient, and very kind.

When people say things like "Champions are champions in their mind first," they're talking about guys like Don. When they say, "Everybody has the will to win but few have the will to prepare to win," they're talking about Don. The best thing I ever heard said about Don was that "nothing is as strong as gentleness, and nothing is as gentle as true strength." It bookends the incredible strength and tender personality of Don; it captures him perfectly.

I muscled up my courage and asked Don if I could come and train with him. A training date was quickly arranged. I couldn't wait! Imagine, a training session with the World's Strongest Man! I was so fired up.

I have never been the same. I believe that there are men God puts in your life, men who change you or the path you're on. Jerry Angelo, the man who recruited me to Syracuse University was one. Jon Kolb, Mike Webster, and of course Tunch Ilkin were others. Joe DeLamielleure, the Hall of Fame guard from the Buffalo Bills and part of the Electric Company that powered O. J. Simpson to the first 2,000-yard rushing season in NFL history, is another man who helped point the way. I also include my high school coaches, Harris Wienke and Bill Caputi, in this revered group. The former taught me how to be a man and take a stand, no matter how unpopular. The latter taught me the basics by which I could feed my family in the years to come. And Carl Battershell, my Syracuse line coach, helped me believe in myself. All of them are great men I thoroughly respect.

But Don was in a category all by himself. I had never seen such monstrous strength as Don possessed. I have never experienced world-class talent coupled with world-class humility as I found in Don. He loved Jesus and could bend steel bars, drive a nail through wood with his bare hand, and blow up a hot water bottle like you would blow up a balloon. And yet he'd rather talk about you than himself. In the world of world champions, they don't make them like Don anymore.

When I first began to train with Don, I was squatting just over 400 pounds. Not exactly mindblowing for somebody weighing 245 to 255 pounds. Alternating sets, we would load Don's barbell up to something over 900 pounds, and then unload mine back down to around 400 pounds. Let me tell you, repetitively lifting and loading five 100-pound plates shoulder height onto a barbell became a little tiring. But that, of course, was just the appetizer. The opportunity to watch a barbell bend over the back and shoulders of a man with trapezius muscles bigger than melons while he squatted up and down with a barbell weighing over 900 pounds was life-changing.

Don had a massive trophy collection, and I would sit and stare at all the trophies and photos after a workout, asking Don all kinds of questions about *this* contest or *that* lift. And Don, bless his heart, sat patiently and answered every question. He was a great role model to all who had the good fortune to cross paths with him. I don't have words enough to tell you what a special man this guy was. I trained with Don for years, and we added training partners as we went along. Two of our partners were high school classmates and teammates on my football team, Jim Burt and Larry Pfohl.

Jim went on to play at the University of Miami (Florida) and won Super Bowls with the New York Giants and San Francisco 49ers. He was also voted to the Pro Bowl in 1986 as a nose tackle. He was strong, tough as nails, and a great competitor.

Pfohl might be better known by his wrestling moniker: Lex Luger. Lex was as big a draw in the wrestling realm of his day as there was. A multiple title holder through the '90s, Larry was strong, had a bodybuilder's physique, and was a great training partner. Without question, he was the best athlete of the three of us.

One day Larry, Jimmy, and I headed down to Don's to work as spotters for him. Believe me, when you are routinely hoisting half a ton of weight on your back, as Don was, you need competent people you can trust as spotters so you don't get hurt. Don was preparing to compete and defend his title in the World's Strongest Man contest. Back then the World's Strongest Man contest was relatively new in the sporting world. It took various competitors from a variety of disciplines—Highland Games athletes, football players, powerlifters, Olympic lifters, wrestlers, field athletes—to compete in various events: pulling a semi truck, the log lift, bending steel bars, those sorts of things.

On this practice day, Don was going to squat. Wearing just a normal wrestling singlet and not all the crazy equipment modern competitors wear to up the poundage of their lifts, Don started to squat, taking his normal, monstrous jumps in between sets. Here was his warm-up routine: he started with 255 pounds for five reps, then jumped to 455 for his second set, followed by increases to 645 and then 765 pounds, all with just one repetition. Don's last warm-up set was 885 pounds for one rep. Conservation of energy was everything. While resting 5 to 10 minutes between each set, his mental concentration was incredible.

I never saw or met anyone as mentally strong and bulletproof as Don Reinhoudt. And on this day, he was about to demonstrate it. When we spotted Don, Jimmy was behind him, while I was at one end of the bar and Larry was at the other end. Not that we were always useful. The man worked out in his garage down in Brocton. It was a small-car garage converted into a gym with carpeting covering the floor. There weren't any safety racks, no power rack that would protect him if he had to dump the bar. One time, Big Don unracked the massive weight, stepped back, and as he did he caught his heel on some loose carpeting and began to wobble, almost stumbling.

Remember, this is 885 pounds sitting on the back of a 365-pound human being. My heart almost stopped! We didn't even attempt to come to his aid because of the enormous weight involved. Doing so would have endangered Don, and, frankly, the weight was just too much. Don somehow, mightily, and with great effort, regained his balance. He steadied himself and began his descent into the bottom position of the squat.

I couldn't believe he had managed to save himself. And then I couldn't believe he was actually going through with the lift. I thought for sure he would have racked it or just dumped it on the floor. Larry, Jimmy, and I were screaming, obviously as encouragement, when it

Posing with my weight lifting idol, Don Reinhoudt.

became apparent that Don would not be deterred. But we were also throwing furtive glances at each other and pushing back our fear and panic. We had just as much fear and panic for ourselves as we did for Don, to be absolutely truthful.

That momentary, heart-palpitating second when it appeared that Don could get hurt made us realize there was nothing we could do had Don been crushed by the weight. In all the years I lifted with Don, so well thought-out were his training cycles, so well did he know himself, and so strong was he, that I had only seen him miss one scheduled lift, and that was a narrow-grip bench press. But he made two out of three reps of 505 pounds!

So Don bottomed out in the squat with that ginormous weight and then slowly reversed the action and began to rise. Remember, this was still just a part of his warm-up! He began shaking as he started to stand up with that massive weight. It was a tough lift all the way around. When he finally stood up and then walked back to the squat stand and racked the weight, there was an enormous sense of relief coursing through his three spotters, who weren't quite so sure of their spotting capabilities at the moment.

Obviously, Don was going to have to wait until the next week, to rest up, and then give the scheduled 965 pounds a whirl. No way could anybody come back from such an energy-sucking, incredibly hard, barely made rep in warm-ups and add nearly 100 pounds to the bar. There was just no way.

Larry, Jimmy, and I—fully aware of the setback in the training cycle and preparation for the World's Strongest Man contest—began to console him as best we could. We all, collectively speaking, knew that humanly speaking, nobody could come back from that near calamity.

Well, except one person. And we were about to get a lesson in the near-supranatural mental, physical, spiritual, and emotional strength of this friendly giant. He was about to demonstrate why he was the reigning strongest man in the world.

Don looked at us as if we had three heads. That is, each of us had three heads. "Please load the bar, fellas," he said without hesitation or doubt. I tried to say something, but one look from Don told me to zip the yapper. (And this, folks, is how world champions are made. They are created with a little more from God than the rest of us mere mortals.)

Don sat calmly and rested for nearly 30 minutes. There was no screaming, bellowing, or histrionics. No, Don was getting ready in his mind. He slugged a little water or Gatorade every now and then, but there was very little conversation.

After loading the barbell to a monstrous 965 pounds, we tightened the collars as best we could. I sat down in fear, curiosity, and amazement. Fear for my friend (not to mention a little trepidation for Jimmy, Larry, and myself in regard to our personal safety), curiosity as to whether or not Don was really going through with the lift, and then amazement that he believed he could lift this massive weight after what had just happened.

But one thing I learned about Don was to never underestimate the competitor in him. He had been through a number of trying exploits, times when he was pushed to the brink of his great strength in competition, and yet another when he saved a life after happening upon a car accident. One of his great attributes was the ability to marshal his inner resources like a Jedi master. To get *Star Wars*–ian on you, Don was Yoda in Chewbacca's body. I had keenly watched Don as he went about his pre-lift mental preparation hundreds of times before, but I had never seen him have to bounce back under such adverse conditions.

Seriously, Don was one of my heroes, a man I admired. So after he gave the thumbs-up and locked in on the 965 pounds, I prayed, willing Don to lift that weight. Nobody wants to see their heroes fail. But I have to admit there was a decided undercurrent of doom and gloom in the stale gym air—at least among the three of us. However, it didn't last for long. Our words of encouragement were met with quick nods of acknowledgment from Don, and then he was lost on another trip into his inner world.

After a while, as Don began to collect his energies, and recycle his mindset, things began to change. And if I hadn't been there personally, if I hadn't experienced this in the flesh, I'm not sure I would have believed it. A very real sense of power and determination began emanating from him. It was almost as if he was a self-generating dynamo. He began to pulsate. In doing so, a vibe of confidence and strength became palpable in the room. So forceful was it, the tendrils of doom and gloom lifted like morning fog under the rising of the sun. Confidence overtook the room. We genuinely began to believe he would lift that weight. As so often when extraordinary moments such as this occur, words fail. You simply had to see it to believe it.

As Don continued to rest, I began to see on the surface the minute twitches and visual cues that belied the deep mental powers he was summoning. His eyes had that distant stare of the man who was now in another realm. My heartbeat quickened as I watched him collect himself. *Surging* is the best word I can come up with to describe the life force that was rising within Don. There was a point at which it became electric. I mean, it was lightning-like. I could see on the faces of Jimmy and Larry that they were feeling it too.

It just couldn't be! We had watched 885 pounds nearly crush Don, and yet the vibe coming off him was a strengthening brace of confidence that was palpable. I could see Don clenching his teeth, the muscles of his jaws and enormous neck flexing. His huge, hamlike fists were squeezing as if he had hold of the bar, then releasing as that inner-world mindset in which he was lost continued to evolve. His eyes flashed and jumped, almost strobe-like. Don was reaching into that inner world in search of a reservoir of untapped strength.

Excitement began to mount within the three of us as we could see Don start his final preparations for the titanic effort this would require. By the time Don got to his feet after wrapping his knees, I had become a believer. Don growled in deep, authoritative tones, telling us to stay out of the way, to not come near the barbell, that it was going to be an all-or-nothing proposition.

No problem there.

Don lightly buckled his powerlifting belt. I remember chalking his back, rubbing the chalk on his massive shoulders so the bar wouldn't slip. We began to verbally get loud, urging him on. The intensity was crackling like the moment before a lightning flash, when your hair stands on end.

Don faced the bar with a fierce look of determination on his face. The moment was upon us. The past 30 minutes were coming together in a kaleidoscope of energies reaching critical mass. I couldn't take my eyes off the man. His was a picture of total and complete concentration. I couldn't swear to the fact that the little gym in Brocton, New York, wasn't registering on a seismograph somewhere. As always with

Don, there was no yelling, no screaming (other than Larry, Jimmy, and me), just 100 percent pure nitro concentration focused with laser-like intensity.

My heart was in my throat. I wanted, *believed*, that Don could succeed, I just couldn't totally convince myself. I kept replaying in my mind the near-catastrophe that 885 pounds had almost wrought. Any such repeat performance with the 965 pounds, and Don would be going to the hospital.

Don stepped under the bar, his face a mask of intensity and fire. Unracking the weight, pausing momentarily to let the bar settle from the bouncing plates that 965 pounds makes. Looking like the mythical Atlas with the world resting on his shoulders, he took two strong, powerful steps back to get into place. A pause, a deep breath, followed by a breathtakingly slow descent.

Don has always been a very controlled lifter. He was a grinder, not explosive. But he would lift with such a commanding presence. He was an overpowering technician who dominated any lift. But at his core, he was just stronger than anybody I've ever met, anybody I've ever seen. It was that simple. Slowly he descended as we bellowed and yelled encouragement. Larry, Jimmy, and I were all scared stiff over what might happen in the next second or two. If you have a muscle blowout or failure in the bottom position with half a ton on your back, it isn't going to end well for you.

He hit the parallel position with us screaming our collective lungs out and...he just stood up. It was jaw-dropping. I have never, ever seen such an incredible display of raw, overwhelming, and concentrated power in my life. It was nearly beyond belief.

As I sit here writing this, I see the lift in my mind's eye. And I remain amazed.

Don racked the bar to a chorus of screaming banshee-like training partners. In his usual fashion, the calmest person in the room was Don.

After unbuckling his belt, Don simply leaned on the bar and smiled. "Thank you," he said in acknowledging the mayhem as we slapped him on the back, screamed, and bellowed. Don wasn't overly demonstrative by any means, but Larry, Jimmy, and I made up for his humility. I think the neighbors were looking out of their front doors to see what all the fuss was about.

Yes, God made Don Reinhoudt with a touch more.

CHAPTER 28

YOI!

There have been a number of significant halftime tributes over the years at Heinz Field that I've been privileged to attend. The tribute to the late Dan Rooney to open the 2017 season is first and foremost. It was very moving, as his passing left all of us with such an overwhelming sense of loss. That sense of loss was pervasive throughout the stadium. The Ambassador, Mr. Rooney, was a giant in life.

My head coach, Chuck Noll, and his wonderful wife, Marianne, coming back to be celebrated was another powerful tribute. It gave me the opportunity to hug Coach one last time. So many captivating memories of him flashed through my mind while he stood at the 50, the overflowing applause from the Heinz Field faithful thundering.

Dick LeBeau being honored in his 50th year in the NFL, with his entire defense standing at rapt attention on the sideline in observance, was incredible. Guys including James Farrior, Brett Keisel, Aaron Smith, Casey Hampton, and Troy Polamalu all looked on in a great show of class and respect.

There was also the night in 2014 against the Ravens when Joe Greene had his No. 75 officially retired. Who can forget the unplanned, unposed, and forever touching and historic photo of Mean Joe and DMR hugging one last time?

And then there was Terry Bradshaw nervously coming back to the 'Burgh in 2002. Pittsburgh stood up and showed how much they loved the Blonde Bomber one more time.

Among these great tributes, allow me to add one more: Monday night, October 31, 2005, when Steelers Nation paid tribute to the Voice of the Steelers himself, Myron Cope. And what better time to salute the diminutive one than on *Monday Night Football*, in Week 8 of the season, against the Baltimore Birdies?

Myron was brought onto the Heinz Field turf twice that night: first for the coin toss and then to address the crowd at halftime. More than 64,000 Steelers fans, Myron Maniacs, roared from the stands and frantically waved their Terrible Towels in a spectacular tribute to the man who invented them. So vociferously and enthusiastically did the towels wave, and in such unison when Myron was introduced at the coin toss, that I, standing on the sideline, could have sworn they kicked up a breeze that night. Let me tell you, this man was truly loved and adored in Pittsburgh. I had been chosen to say a word or two of introduction for Myron when he came out for the halftime tribute. I felt truly honored to be there, and I said so to my good friend, Tony Quatrini, head of Steelers marketing, who had asked me to do it.

Cope came to the sideline just before halftime. The crowd was cheering, revving up for Myron. The players were just getting off the field and the security and grounds crew were moving quickly into place. As Cope was escorted onto the field for the second time that night and moved into position, you could feel the anticipation rippling through the crowd. Fans were genuinely gonzo for his appearance. Let me put it this way: few had left for their halftime bathroom break.

Tony handed me the microphone, pulled me close, and said, "Now listen: this is important. You know how Cope likes to talk. When I give you the sign to get Myron off the field, you have to make sure you get him off the field. The NFL fines you a ton of money for every minute you run over at halftime."

"Whoa, whoa, whoa," I replied. "Tony, wait a minute. Halftime is only 12 minutes long. Myron's only getting warmed up at 12 minutes. What if he runs over?"

"I don't care if you have to tackle him and wrestle for the microphone. He's got to come off the field when I tell you."

I stared at Tony, slightly dumbfounded. The full implication of what he said was just registering. "Great," I said, "I'm the guy who'll be remembered for tackling Myron and wrestling him for the mic."

"Why do you think I asked you to do it?" Tony said, laughing. I started laughing too. Laughing like I did when I was a kid scared out of my wits, like the time I bet a friend I'd walk through a cemetery at night. Laughing like I was about to rocket out of the starting gate at Kennywood on a roller coaster. I guess a little hysteria is good for the soul. Then a thought suddenly washed over me: a 300-pound me chasing and wrestling to the ground the 5'2", *maybe* 130-pounds-soaking-wet Myron Cope.

It wasn't just my sense of humor that was mounting. There was a simultaneous sense of terror along with it. And what about the ESPN highlights? It would traumatize the city for years!

I looked at Tony, searching for an out. But the Jumbotron highlight reel was over, and suddenly it was time. I turned and walked onto the field, introduced Myron, and the legend took over. Myron warmed into the tribute, took his time, and all the while I nervously looked from Tony to Cope to the ever-present Heinz Field clock ticking away on the scoreboard. And then back again.

It turns out I should never have given it a second thought. After all of that worry, Cope was spectacular, as only he can be. His class was extraordinary on this extraordinary night. With the crowd roaring, Myron alternately had them cheering, smiling, laughing, and probably crying. Myron demonstrated better clock management than a Ben Roethlisberger two-minute drill in taking the clock down to the prearranged deadline.

As halftime came ticking to a close, he signed off and promptly handed over the microphone. Myron left the field to the cheers of thousands, as timeless as the hypocycloids on the Steelers' helmets.

Yoi!

And double that for me.

CHAPTER 29

WHEN COACHES LIE

First of all, I harbor great love and appreciation for all of the coaches who have directly—and even indirectly—influenced or played a role in my career, regardless of how much or how little. Truly.

But...

They lie.

First I'm going to tell you about my senior year at Syracuse University. It was a humid training-camp day in the summer of 1979, heading into my senior season. And I had just accomplished something I had wanted to accomplish since my freshman year: I busted the two-man sled. All by my lonesome. I'd hit that rusty old thing so many times over the years that I had become obsessed with a white-hot, fervent desire to mulch that piece of crap. And my day of vengeance finally arrived on this sweltering August day.

After stretching and team starts, we broke off into individual period, in which the offensive line would work by itself in a group setting. As part of the individual period, there was the daily battle with the two-man blocking sled. Oh, how I hated that thing. It seemed to mock me, standing there, all rusted up, just a lowlife piece of junk metal. Our offensive line coach would stand on the sled part as we slammed into that old rust bucket over and over again until exhaustion set in. Our line coach would have us drive-block that junk for 10 to 15 seconds of continuous, all-out effort. It was like trying to sprint while pushing a car as someone tapped the brakes over and over again. My line coach, complete with whistle, would yell, curse, and belittle our efforts. It was a daily battle with the most devious, hateful inanimate object I'd ever experienced in my life.

So there I was, for the umpteenth time in my collegiate career, ready to engage in mortal combat yet again. I took a quick swig of water, buckled my chinstrap, and stepped into position. Easing into my three-point stance, I paused as my heart hammered away in my chest. I sucked in a final breath of hot, humid air and focused on the whistle. At the shrill sound, I blasted out of my stance with a flat back, rolled over my front foot, and made a textbook-style drive block. My hips engaged and I ripped to rack, punching hard with my glove-covered fists into the padded exterior as my shoulder pads slammed into that sled. With a tremendous *crack!* the rusted, twisted metal gave way. Lo and behold, it began to crumple…and then it buckled!

Oh, I rose triumphantly to my feet! Fists clenched overhead, laughing uproariously at my sudden good fortune, I began to walk toward the gate of the surrounding fence at the practice field. Oh, sweet mother of pearl! I was done for the day and I wanted everybody to notice. I was heading for the showers! I hated that two-man sled. *Despised* it. We hit it every dadgum practice, and my line coach had a standing promise to all of his offensive linemen: If anyone broke the sled from a hit, they would have the rest of practice off. And baby, I meant to collect on that promise, beginning right now!

My line coach began yelling at me to come back. Delirious as I was, from dehydration, heat, humidity, and the supramaximal effort it took to break that stupid sled, I was confounded. It didn't help that I could hardly hear him because I was huffing like an old steam engine going up a mountain.

"Whaddaya mean, come back?"

My O-line coach quickly threw a bucket of ice-cold nope on me and my promised day off. And I looked at him as if he had three heads. I could not comprehend that he was reneging on a promise. So, yes, coaches lie! For three years I had heard that repeated promise of a day off if I could manage to do what I had just done. And now…

Fast-forward a few years to one of Chuck Noll's camps. To put it mildly, they weren't very fun. As a matter of fact, they were pretty brutal. The heat, humidity, and violence of full-go padded practices twice a day were followed by conditioning. It was more than enough misery to melt even the most battle-hardened veteran.

Coaches, of course, need to motivate their players. Steelers linemen (left to right) me, John Jackson (65), and Tunch Ilkin (62) with OL coach Ron Blackledge. Courtesy of the Pittsburgh Steelers

Coach knew that even Hall of Fame players had their limits. And sometimes dangling a carrot of a promise out there was deemed appropriate. But Coach Noll had a way of making mirages out of promises.

One day, when the thermometer was toying with the idea of the upper 90s, along with the humidity that shrouded the Laurel Mountains in morning fog, Coach addressed the team: "We want to get on the field, get our business done as quickly as possible, and get off the field. It's going to be very hot, so let's concentrate and hustle and shorten our practice time."

Now that sounded so, so good as I sat there in the meeting room before practice. In fact, it sounded too good to be true. And if it sounds too good to be true, it probably is. And it was. Two hours and 25 minutes later, we were all wondering about that plan to cut into a two-hour practice. Because coaches lie.

Here I sit, years after my last professional practice, reading a news article that verified what we as players had always suspected. Suspected? No, what we *knew*. It has been researched and *verified*, with independent testing protocols, that bending over with your hands on your knees is the best possible posture to help in recovering from a strenuous effort. Bending over helps to speed the recuperative process! It says right here that it allows the respiratory system the fastest route of recovery. Now imagine that!

Fellas, coaches lied to us about this for years. I can't count the number of times while playing in any competitive environment that I was told, "There's no air down there."

Seriously, I had been reprimanded too many times for gasping for air while bent over. My coaches told me to "Stand tall!" Over and over.

The thing was, we all *knew* there was air down there. We *knew* that standing tall didn't help us recover as fast as being hunched over, sobbing for air and maybe even puking a little. And yet, here we are today, with academic guys having actually researched it and put it in this definitive paper I'm holding right here in my hand that says otherwise. Think about it. You're in the huddle waiting for the next play, or listening for the whistle to run the next sprint, and all this time you've wasted your energy standing tall when you could've been recuperating. Yeah, it's a miserable business—especially when the very people you, as an athlete, have trusted instead fail you.

Coaches lie. And they always will.

CHAPTER 30

THE LEGEND OF FATS

The Steelers have employed a number of great and legendary players throughout their history, which began in 1933. You can look up the Hall of Famers and read about the legends. Others have had their stories passed down by other players, such as the legendary exploits of the great defensive tackle of the 1970s, Ernie "Fats" Holmes.

I had seen the picture and noticed the arrow shaved in the top of his head. Ernie "Arrowhead" Holmes! He told teammates it was pointing the way to the Super Bowl. And he was right. I remembered that picture because I actually had the same thing shaved into my head by some older teammates in my freshman year at Syracuse University. (Hey, they might have been Ernie Holmes fans!) But you should've seen the look of disbelief on my mother's face when I showed up at home, freshly shorn.

I had seen Ernie play in the '70s, so it was cool to hear the stories about him when I joined the team alongside some of his former teammates. Holmes had retired before I arrived. He played 84 games and recorded 39.5 sacks with the Steelers for six years and the Patriots in his final season. But those are only the cold, hard statistics of a man whose ability to intimidate opponents was on par with that of Joe Greene and Jack Lambert, and more modern players such as Greg Lloyd and James Harrison.

Certainly, when Ernie was playing his best ball he was an intimidating force, a player against whom even the toughest and most hardened of opponents did not want to spend an NFL afternoon scrapping. He had such an intimidating and fearsome reputation that nobody wanted to fight him either. However—and this totally caught me by surprise—I heard talk from some of the older guys that he was actually a kind-hearted, gentle guy. There was something about him that everybody liked. He would dress up as Santa Claus for team parties and buy toys with his own money for the kids of his teammates.

Frankly, trying to marry the two very different sides of Ernie Holmes was confusing, even when I met him in person. I had that opportunity way back in the early 1980s. I remember stepping off the team bus with Tunch Ilkin and Mike Webster and squinting. I had to shield my eyes against the bright Southern California sun. We trudged toward the stadium for practice during the final days of preparation for our playoff game in Los Angeles on New Year's Day 1984.

We'd had a good season in 1983. We had been 9–2 before skidding late and ending up 10–6. We won only one of our last five regular-season games. The Browns and Bengals stayed close on our heels, but we managed to keep it together and win the division. The Raiders, meanwhile, came into the playoff game with a 12–4 record and awaited us at Memorial Coliseum. (Spoiler alert: it was these same Raiders who would go on to win in the Super Bowl in a rout of the Washington Redskins.)

We landed in L.A. several days early and stayed in Thousand Oaks, California, where the Dallas Cowboys held their training camps until 1989. After several days in Thousand Oaks, we headed for the big city and spent the night before the game in downtown L.A. on New Year's Eve. We were there because the weather back in Pittsburgh was freezing, and (thankfully) the higher-ups felt it necessary for us to get acclimated to SoCal. I certainly don't remember anyone on the team in disagreement. We were suffering the aftereffects of a rough 16-game season that left many of us with a bit of a hitch in our get-along. That warm sun was just what the doctor ordered for a weary and battered team. We hoped that it would rejuvenate us before the playoffs.

Now remember, this was back in the day when it was customary to practice in pads three times a week, excepting game day. And I might also add, in those three practices we went full-go. It was "bump" on the backs—as in you couldn't hit Franco or Terry—but for the rest of us slobs it was as close to game speed as we could get, without the wanton violence of actual game speed. Though I can honestly say that I have played some games that were easier than some of our practices.

As we entered into the gated area and headed to the locker room, I noticed an immense human being standing just inside the gate. He was shaking hands with some, hugging others. The man was *huge*. I'm guessing he was 375 to 400 pounds on a 6'3" frame. I stopped for a moment and tried to figure out who he was. Though he wasn't in playing shape, you could tell that at one time he was probably a powerful athlete. I could see some of the players smiling and talking, and I was obviously struck by his size. But the closer I got, the more I saw the fearsome look of the man. Then somebody said, "Hey! That's Ernie Holmes!"

Ernie Holmes. *Wow.* I had heard his stories ever since I had come to Pittsburgh. He was a legendary character. Ernie Holmes, the man who engaged in fierce training-camp battles with Mike Webster! Ernie Holmes, who gleefully came back into the huddle after a play he had screwed up because he was out to get retribution on a guy! That guy was none other than Hall of Fame Raiders guard Gene Upshaw. Those two, it was said, had a running battle each time they played. In fact, when Ernie got back to the huddle, he breathlessly told Andy Russell, who was berating Ernie for forsaking his assignment, "But I got him, Andy!" (Of course Andy knew how far to take it with Ernie and let the matter drop until he had more backup on the sideline.)

Yes, this was the same Ernie Holmes who had a psychotic episode in the spring of 1973 that resulted in guns, a high-speed police chase, and Ernie shooting at a police helicopter. The result of that episode was time in a psychiatric ward. After Ernie was released, when he was at training camp the following summer, one of the TV stations in Pittsburgh flew its chopper out to St. Vincent College. When the chopper flew over the practice field, L. C. Greenwood said, "Easy, Fats," as teammates erupted in laughter.

Yes, Ernie Holmes, the defensive tackle about whom Mike Wagner once opined, "He had a look that was really scary. I think he wanted to beat people to death—within the rules of the game."

Ernie was driven to succeed, and this pushed him to go all out on every play, whether it was practice or a game. Every time the ball was snapped and he didn't win at the whistle, he felt it was a threat to his career. The ferocious attitude with which he played and practiced welled up from deep inside. It was as if there was an internal angst, an anger, that unmercifully drove him. Something growled from deep down and expressed itself at the next snap of the ball. "I don't know what my life is," he once told *Time* magazine, "except there's something pounding in the back of my head."

Yes, it was *that* Ernie Holmes. So many other stories rolled around in my mind in that moment that I felt the urge to pause and simply take in the man. And frankly, there was no way to get around him. He was the perfect four-by-four square peg who would ram himself into a round hole if needed. He had positioned himself such that you would have to go by him to pass through the gate.

I certainly was intrigued and wanted to meet this man about whom I had heard so much. I decided to introduce myself and warily approached and stuck out my hand. "Hi, Ernie! Craig Wolfley. Glad to meet you."

Ernie pulled me in closely, momentarily, and looked directly into my eyes. Those eyes of his, I'm telling you, were piercing and intense. Very intense. Shark Week intense. As if to further intensify the moment, his grip tightened, serving as a powerful reminder of the physical strength he not only once possessed but still did. We talked for a moment before I excused myself to get ready for practice.

To this day—and I'm not sure if it was his grip, his piercing eyes, or the stories swirling in my head—I felt slightly uneasy coming into close contact with the man. And as far as the legends go, I am a believer. The longer we talked, the more I came to believe most, if not all, of those stories. They ranged from wildly comedic to super intense, from revenge-oriented actions to acts of great generosity and kindness. All the while, he was described as a great teammate.

There's the hilarious story of Ernie grabbing Myron Cope in the hallway of the team hotel the night before a game. Ernie told Cope that he needed to come and have a drink with him. Of course Myron, not one to pass up a toddy, happily obliged. But as Myron would say later, "If Fats asked me to go and get a colonoscopy with him, I was in no position to say no."

Ernie once threw himself a bachelor party, and it was through his sheer force of personality that defensive members of the Steelers were "invited" to attend. I'll leave the rest of that story to your imagination. It's Steelers legend.

One time in training camp, Ernie had a headache and told defensive line coach George Perles that he couldn't practice and sat down on his helmet—I mean, right in the middle of a drill Perles was conducting! George, knowing Ernie's explosive personality, simply moved the drill about 20 yards away. Ernie, Steelers legend has it, simply sat there on his helmet and glared at everybody.

A guy once relayed a story of when he was a young man who had worked a party at a bar that Perles threw for his defensive linemen. It was complete with a huge buffet, including a stuffed pig. After eating a considerable amount, Ernie grabbed the pig's head, cracked it open, and ate the brain. Remember, though, Ernie was a Texan, and that might be a delicacy in the Lone Star State for all I know. Hey, to each his own.

Talk about delicacies reminds me of my own brush with offal (or is it awful?). While on a ski trip to Montana once, I attended a cowboy buffet and came upon a delicacy called Rocky Mountain oysters. After hesitating, I stuck my plate out for a serving. Before he dished out a couple "oysters," the server asked to hear my accent, since he knew I might not have the stomach for deep-fried bull testicles.

Anyway, yes, it was this Ernie Holmes with whom I shook hands and kibitzed for a moment. After saying goodbye, I went to the locker room. On my way, I fell in step with Tunch and said, "You know all those stories we heard about Ernie?" Tunch looked at me and we stopped. "They're all true!" I said with conviction. Looking into Ernie's eyes, shaking his hand, listening to him talk, they all combined to solidify everything I had heard about Ernie; the good, the bad, the ugly.

But this wasn't the end of the story of Ernie Holmes. Though Fats had rough times and suffered from some mental health issues, he was loved by most of his teammates. Yes, he was a walking powder keg in his young days, but he also became a two-time Super Bowl champion as well. After his troublesome years, Ernie found the Lord; yes, proving that God is a God of forgiveness, a God of second, third, and multiple chances, always ready to forgive, to share His grace with the repentant. And Ernie's life swung completely around. At the time of his death, he was a pastor of a church in his home state of Texas.

I last saw Ernie at a Steelers alumni function many years later at Heinz Field. The man whom I had met way back in 1983 in L.A. was totally different, a man changed by the grace of God. And as I stood there and watched him interact with others, a deep feeling of respect washed over me. As we shook hands and exchanged greetings—he with that same powerful handshake, same deep voice and piercing eyes—I couldn't help but notice the new foundation of the peace of God undergirding him "that passes all understanding."

Ernie Holmes passed away in 2008. But with his passing went the trail of stories that truly spoke of a fearsome player; an enforcer, as some of his teammates described him; and an integral part of the Steel Curtain. He was a beloved teammate as well, a guy many said was simply misunderstood.

CHAPTER 31

RECIPE OF A FOOTBALL LIFE

The game of football has been a singular, lifelong pursuit of happiness for me. It has given me so much more than I could possibly have imagined, starting from my most humble beginnings on a small, rutted, and slightly grassy field in Orchard Park so many years ago. I'm so very grateful for the opportunities that have been afforded to me in playing this great game.

I was drawn to the sport from the very beginning. The sheer chaos and violence spoke to me as a young guy who grew up in a small, brethren assembly, where "turning the other cheek" was a way of life that a person who sought to follow hard after Jesus took to heart. To find a sport in which I didn't need to turn the other cheek, but instead could join in on the high-velocity collisions and do so joyfully? That was everything to me.

My first experience in organized football occurred at Orchard Park Junior High School. It was intramural football, meaning it was within the confines of school and played after school. It was prep for freshman football. There comes a time when you realize that maybe, just maybe, you were cut out for the life you sought. Mine might have come here.

I was on the junior varsity squad during an intermingled practice with the varsity guys. I remember being so in awe of those guys and loved the feeling of hanging with the big boys. When it came time to test my skills, as limited and unimpressive as they were at this point, it felt like an all-or-nothing moment in front of the boys and the coaches. It was the Bull in the Ring drill. I felt all eyes on me while I nervously stepped into the middle. It was a conditioning drill, a learning drill, and a big stage on which I was first introduced to peer pressure. It was also the beginning of my real football education.

Bull in the Ring was a precursor to Backs on Backers and the infamous Oklahoma drill—drills that, for the most part, have gone the way of bell-bottoms and eight-tracks. It is very simple and very instructive. One guy stands in the middle of a circle of players, maybe five yards or

During my senior season at Syracuse University, with QB Bill Hurley (5) and LB Jim Collins (33). Hurley and I were drafted in back-to-back rounds by the Steelers in 1980. Courtesy of Syracuse University

so away from each. The coach calls out a name, and that player tries to run over the guy in the middle. The player in the middle has to quickly identify the rusher, get into a hitting posture, and simultaneously deliver a blow to neutralize being hit while not getting knocked out of position. Individually, each aspect involves a valuable trait to be learned and then used to protect oneself on the field.

I still remember the inner glow I felt when the toughest kid out there back in those Orchard Park days, Jackie Smith, couldn't knock me over or out of the middle position. Jackie was older than me by a couple of years, an excellent ballplayer who everybody feared, especially me. When Coach Wienke called his name while I was the bull, I thought I was dead meat. Seriously! But when the dust settled after a wicked collision, somehow there I stood, with all my fellow young bucks looking at me in amazement. I tried to hide the fact that I was more amazed than any of them that I was still standing. That's when something in me clicked. Just as I *knew* that I wanted to pursue a career in football, I also knew deep down that I had just passed my first real test.

And that's what football really is: a day-to-day test of your desire and ability to overcome. Being a big fish in a small pond is one thing. Heading out to test yourself in deeper waters is another thing altogether. My deeper waters had their beginnings in the spring of my senior year in high school, when I accepted a scholarship to Syracuse University. I was then blessed to be picked to play in a summer All-Star Classic held at the University of Buffalo along with the top players in western New York back in 1976. Those were my first steps in learning where I stood in the pecking order of tough guys.

I was on my way to learning three truths: yoga pants don't lie, neither do young kids, and neither does the Oklahoma drill. The Oklahoma is the roughest one-on-one drill I ever encountered, the one that really started to separate the pecking order of alpha males. That began to take shape my freshman year at Syracuse. The drill was first introduced by legendary

Oklahoma coach Bud Wilkinson. It consists of two heavy bags, usually those used so players can learn the proper blocking form while not taking any extra hits. The idea is to put an offensive lineman on one side of a scrimmage line and between the bags, and then a defensive lineman directly over him. About five yards behind the offensive lineman, a quarterback has a football, and about three yards behind the QB is a running back. The two heavy bags are about five yards apart. At the snap, the QB hands to the RB, who has to hit it up between the two heavy bags. The offensive lineman must drive-block the defensive lineman, or the defensive lineman has to neutralize the block, disengage, defeat it, and tackle the RB when he tries to run by. It's a high-velocity collision drill and the learning curve is tremendous. It really separates those who are *driven* to play ball from those who merely *like* to play ball.

Funnily, Coach Wienke, whom I idolized and can never thank enough for teaching me the fundamentals, would occasionally jump into the fray when we were freshmen in high school and go one-on-one with us. Harris Wienke had been an offensive lineman on the Syracuse University team, a big guy back in the day. And he'd jump in without pads, not even a helmet. Coach Wienke and assistant coach Bill Caputi were the two biggest influences in my young life. And I thank them both for teaching me the fundamentals that ultimately allowed me to feed my family.

As always, with each step up in competition, there are the moments when you have to stand before all of your coaches and teammates and show that you're capable. While the dynamics might change and the level of competition may change, the emphasis is always about the building blocks that make an offensive or defensive lineman.

During my first college training camp at Syracuse, I watched while standing in line and waiting my turn. I was so anxious to come out of the gates hot, to show my peers and the upperclassmen that I was capable of playing with the big boys. Being a freshman, I was naturally near the back of the line, but I made sure to grab a good vantage point to watch the madness that the Oklahoma drill can elicit. I remember watching Bill Varvari, the starting center, line up against Syracuse all-time great defensive tackle Ken Clarke, who would go on to play 14 seasons in the NFL. Kenny had a flipper to be feared. He could destroy you with an incredibly powerful forearm to the helmet. Kenny was a stud. Thick of neck and impressively strong, he was a guy who literally could destroy you.

Kenny slid into his stance easily as Varvari took his position across the line of scrimmage. The cadence, the snap, and the *wham!* seemed almost simultaneous. It was a thunderous hit, and quite frankly, it shocked me. I'd never seen such power displayed in so destructive a manner in such a short, limited space. Kenny literally knocked Varvari to his knees as a general wave of awe swept over the area before the coaches jumped in with commentary and teaching techniques. All I could remember was thinking, *I'm not ready for this!*

Varvari, a tough guy himself, shook off a little grogginess, rotated to the back of the line, and then it was the next two guys' turn. One by one the lines diminished as guys took their turns in trying to outdo each other. And one by one, I inched closer to being the next man up. I got the snap count, took my place, and mustered whatever courage I had left, because a good deal of it had left me when Kenny took down Bill. Drawing in all I could, I shot off the ball at the snap. Though it wasn't pretty, I did all right. More importantly, I survived. I don't remember my opponent, but it didn't matter. I was excited to have had my first real taste of D-1 competition.

You're doggone right I took my lumps along the way, but I kept at it and I learned. And eventually I got better. If it hadn't been for the Oklahoma drill, and others like it, I don't know how far I would have gone. Those drills were crucial to building what was necessary before I landed in Pittsburgh.

Nowadays, NFL training camps have been whittled down to a long weekend. In fact, the Collective Bargaining Agreement allows five single-practice days with limited contact and then a mandated day off. Oklahoma drills are not allowed. I wouldn't be surprised if Backs on Backers soon follows suit.

One-on-one pass-rush drills, the backbone of learning to pass protect and pass rush, are limited to one big move by a pass rusher and then stop. Back in the day, it went on until one man was standing. Why was it important to be the last man standing? Because the process gives players an opportunity to work their way out of possibly bad pass-rush positions. In a game, you can't simply stop or give up just because you're going backward at an accelerated rate due to a strong bull rush. You have to learn how to stuff a bull rush. And trust me, no quarterback wants to be in a game with an offensive lineman who's just then learning how to stuff a bull rush.

Learning to quickly give ground with a short hop and then a strong plant, using your legs, and then stuffing the bull rush by regaining the under-and-up leverage while locking out at arm's length is an art form all its own. But it's got to be trained in the moment. At high intensity. You can't virtual-reality your way into stuffing a bull rush from a 350-pounder. You have to experience it and learn to execute your technique while he's trying to squash you in real time. And by the way, the headbutt-first bull rush is no longer an acceptable pass-rushing technique. There's a new millennial, hands-first bull-rush technique that players must learn to defend. If you want to see it in action, defensive tackle extraordinaire Cam Heyward of the Steelers is the very best technician of the one-arm-stab/bull-rush technique in the modern era.

Yes, football is a game with an elevated risk level. There's an injury potential ranging from "that hurts" to the devastating. I understand those sentiments, believe me. But all of life is a risk. This game is a great game. I hope those, in trying to make the game safer, take into account that limited bouts of hard contact are still the best way to stay safe. Limit the high-velocity, high-intensity, full-contact drills but don't eliminate them, because they have great value.

Team drills, when you run plays at almost full go, also provide the necessary testing and strengthening of important ligaments in a player's body. They also teach a player to develop his samurai sixth sense, to go with the blow or to fight the driving force on you, or learn how to protect yourself in the middle of the scrum. Nothing teaches you like life in the trenches.

CHAPTER 32

THE PARTY BUS

Tunch laughed when he said that one enters broadcasting when one has no other marketable skills.

Marketable or not, life as a broadcaster for the Steelers Radio Network is just plain fun. Week in and week out, one of the most enjoyable aspects of the job is that I'm afforded the opportunity to meet and greet Steelers fans across the country. Whether in person or via the airwaves, I get the privilege of chatting up some of the world's most interesting people.

It might be a caller from Chicago such as Steeler Jimmy, or it might be Alan from across the Atlantic in Dublin, Ireland, from where we also catch up on some of the latest cricket news. There's Tiny Dancer, otherwise known as Elton, from Virginia; we discuss how to best "mojinate" for the game. Jocko, Cujo, or one of my personal favorites, the Sarcastic Sword, all have something to say, a point to get across, or the need to vent a little because nobody on the home front might be listening. Whether the caller and I squabble, or whether the new friend and I are about to shake hands, it's always enjoyable because of our common interest in all things Steelers.

There were times when you might have caught me and Tunch walking about the city—"urban hiking," as Tunch called it, while "forced death march" was my interpretation. One night before a game in New Orleans, we lapped the French Quarter and talked with Steelers fans about the game.

Along with the prospect of encountering Steelers Nation on a walkabout, there are the entertaining Steelers fans at a sponsors' dinner the night before an out-of-town game, with a calorie slaughter of magnificent proportion on full display. The routine of traveling Steelers-style is pretty simple. On Saturday, show up at the airport, grab some grub, and get on the plane. After landing in the scheduled city, board a bus on the tarmac, take the bus straight to the hotel (complete with a police escort), and check in to the hotel via lobby tables full of room keys and smiling

My mother, Hoopy, was so proud of me for my deeds both on the field and off. The Chief, Art Rooney, expressed those same feelings of pride in this letter.

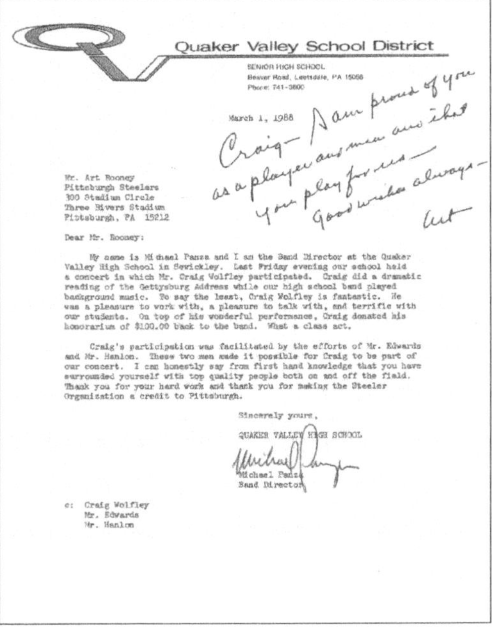

Quaker Valley School District

SENIOR HIGH SCHOOL
Beaver Road, Leetsdale, PA 15056
Phone: 741-3800

March 1, 1988

Craig— I am proud of you as a player and man and that you play for us— Good wishes always— Art

Mr. Art Rooney
Pittsburgh Steelers
300 Stadium Circle
Three Rivers Stadium
Pittsburgh, PA 15212

Dear Mr. Rooney:

My name is Michael Panza and I am the Band Director at the Quaker Valley High School in Sewickley. Last Friday evening our school held a concert in which Mr. Craig Wolfley participated. Craig did a dramatic reading of the Gettysburg Address while our high school band played background music. To say the least, Craig Wolfley is fantastic. He was a pleasure to work with, a pleasure to talk with, and terrific with our students. On top of his wonderful performance, Craig donated his honorarium of $100.00 back to the band. What a class act.

Craig's participation was facilitated by the efforts of Mr. Edwards and Mr. Hanlon. These two men made it possible for Craig to be part of our concert. I can honestly say from first hand knowledge that you have surrounded yourself with top quality people both on and off the field. Thank you for your hard work and thank you for making the Steeler Organization a credit to Pittsburgh.

Sincerely yours,

QUAKER VALLEY HIGH SCHOOL

Michael Panza
Band Director

c: Craig Wolfley
Mr. Edwards
Mr. Hanlon

hotel personnel pointing you to the elevators. And then you can kick back in your private room. Seriously, it's like hitting the EASY button when you travel.

The night before a game is always fun. The Steelers bring along sponsors on these trips and entertain clients. It's just good business to take the clients along on a road trip, feed them at an outstanding restaurant the night before a game, feed them again at breakfast in the same room as the players, and then take them to the game complete with Steelers marketing escorts.

My role is to go along with the group to tell war stories, and to answer questions about the next day's game. Of course for me, it's all about the food. As a lifelong fat guy at heart—someone Tunch once referred to as "the man who did for food what Dean Martin did for alcohol"—new restaurants and five-star eating are absolute highlights.

One particular weekend. the Steelers headed to Buffalo to take on my hometown Bills in a regular-season game. Happily, coming back to Buffalo always meant seeing my mom. Known as Hoopy to her great-grandkids, grandkids, and we kids, Esther Carol Wolfley-Randall was the centerpiece and glowing light of all things growing up Wolfley. She's a shining example of a godly woman who epitomizes a servant's attitude and extends love to all—including my late and great, lifelong brother, teammate, and friend Tunch. She often referred to him as one of her sons. Faith's and my fifth child, Esther Lou, is named after Mom, and it is because of the great love that Hoopy has inspired and spread throughout the entire Wolfley clan that "Esty Lou," as Hoopy happily calls her namesake, was so named.

Well, the only foreseeable problem with my marketing duties on this particular trip to Buffalo was that I needed to be at the restaurant, and therefore my mom time was in danger. For a lot of other teams, this would be a problem. But it was no problem as far as Steelers marketing people Tony Quatrini and Rick Giugliano were concerned. They instructed me just to bring Hoopy and my stepdad, Tom Randall, along with the crew. They would be welcomed with open arms.

We set it all up, and after an ever-joyous greeting from my mom at the hotel, introductions were made around the lobby. My mom soon unleashed the storyteller in her—which, as you might expect, always includes embarrassing stories about yours truly—and soon it was time to set off for the restaurant.

On this cold night in Buffalo (redundant, I know), our entourage of 15 to 20 people required a bus instead of a taxi. In fact, we needed a big bus. Naturally, travel arrangements had been scheduled well in advance and the duly ordered bus was assigned sight unseen. The bus arrived and we boarded en masse. After taking our seats, I realized this wasn't a normal bus. For one, the seats all faced each other along the interior, and then there were disco-like lights spaced about the bus, with a pole

Wolf List: My Top 10 Most Favorite Foods

My voracious appetite was well-known among my teammates, but hey, I knew how to eat! Here is my official Mount Rushmore of foods.

10. Hyde Park Prime Steakhouse's 40-ounce Coach Tomlin Steak.
9. Fat Guy Delight from Sharky's Café in Latrobe, PA.
8. Stuffed Hot Banana Peppers from Pizzaz in McMurray, PA.
7. Sarafino's Pasta Speciale in Crafton, PA.
6. Porky's Revenge Pizza from Caliente Pizza & Drafthouse.
5. Sushi (preferably the all-you-can-eat variety).
4. Robin's No-Bake Cookies.
3. Aunt Nellie's Blueberry Pie.
2. Grandma Lamb's homemade "Birthday" Cherry Pie.
1. Hoopy's Iced Oatmeal Cookies.

prominently displayed in the center. It appeared to have a wooden dance floor. No, this was definitely not your average people-moving transport bus.

Tony Q and Googs looked at each other with raised eyebrows, and we all kind of laughed when it became obvious that this was a bus more suited for bachelor and bachelorette parties than a family night out with sponsors. But apparently this was the only bus available to transport a group this size. "Well," as I told Tunch, "at least it's heated."

The rest of the group fell into silence. Quizzical expressions floated throughout the circle. Hushed voices mixed with spurts of giggles and snorts from those who had just made the connection. I tried not to let on what I was thinking. I could only imagine what my mom was thinking as she sat next to me. I didn't have to wait long. Tunch nudged me in the ribs and whispered, "Look at Hoopy."

Mom was sitting to my right and looking at the garish lights, bold colors, *Saturday Night Fever*-style disco ball hanging in the center, and of course the pole and dance floor. I could see the wheels turning in her head. It's important to understand that my mom had been a country gal for nearly 30 years since she remarried following my dad's passing. And it was obvious that she was confused by the whole thing. Hoopy had her hand by her mouth, her lips pursed in a questioning posture—always a dead giveaway to the rest of us that she was troubled and in deep thought. I could see she was trying to come up with an explanation of what this bus was all about. Now, put her on *The Partridge Family* bus and she's right at home, but this?

Hoopy's eyes darted from one side of the bus to the other, yet after watching out of the corner of my eye for a moment, I could see she would always end up centrally locating her gaze. To be more specific, it was obvious that she couldn't comprehend why there was a pole in the center of the bus. After a few moments of concentrated study, chatter arose as everyone became used to the bus. That's when Hoopy leaned close to me and said in a low voice, "Honey, why is there a pole in the middle of the bus?"

Tunch's eyebrows immediately pulled together into his infamous unibrow, the appearance of which generally meant he was either angry or on the brink of busting a gut in laughter. After elbowing me several times, Tunch tried rather unsuccessfully to stifle a laugh, as I caught the can't-wait-to-hear-this look on his face. So he leaned in to hear my thoughtful answer. "Safety first, Hoopy," I said with a straight face. "Overcrowding on a public bus, without something to hang on to, can be dangerous."

"Oh," she said, sounding unconvinced.

That's my story, Mom. And I stuck to it.

CHAPTER 33

SAMURAI SIXTH SENSE

Instinct. Like all animals, we humans have it. We are hardwired genetically with different behaviors that enhance our ability to cope with various environmental contingencies, even on the football field.

Instinct. It's that gut reaction to a person, circumstance, or place. In the world of professional football, I refer to it as "game brains." It's the concentration of all of your football experiences poured into your player tank, which you draw from during the course of a game. For most mortals, the X's and O's of the playbook are just that. But the great players seem to operate on an extra dimension where the X's and O's start moving. From the ancient samurai to today's modern warfighters and the athletes of today, there exists a visceral inner reaction to a set of circumstances, people, or places, which then dictates a variable real-world response. It's a necessary part of every athlete's tool kit. And that was a just a long, descriptive way of saying "just trust your gut."

Now, I love reading about the samurai of feudal Japan. Courageous, loyal, and powerful, the warlike samurai never retired. Their fighting techniques are pretty much akin to a Darwinian "thinning the herd" concept. If one of their techniques in fighting worked, the samurai survived and added it to his skill set. If the technique failed, he most likely died and the failed technique died with him.

Woven throughout samurai lore is the acknowledged "knowing" of the battle-worn samurai. He gains the skill of *mushin*, learning to turn off the internal chatter and concentrate, and also *zanshin*, alertness distilled to its essence. We Americans might know it better as sixth sense, or being in the zone. Sensing rather than thinking, flowing rather than planning, understanding the opponent, circumstance, and situation with an inner vibe that can't be equivocated into words. You just do it, all while having the courage to ride with that decision, and possibly face repercussions if you are wrong.

I've often heard great players, while making great plays, in private acknowledge that they weren't sure why they did what they did. But they did. Because they just knew. I love it.

Andy Russell once told me the story of Joe Greene, in the huddle during a critical part of the game, telling everybody in no uncertain terms that he was going to take the ball away from the Oilers on the next play. And he did. Joe just *knew* it.

Of course, things don't always go your way, but you have to own it. I remember back in 1984, playing the Raiders in the Coliseum. In the huddle during a stoppage in play, quarterback Cliff Stoudt came back

Wolf List: The 10 Greatest Plays I Ever Saw

The Pittsburgh Steelers have more than their fair share of famous plays (the Immaculate Reception, anyone?). Here are the 10 best I was fortunate enough to witness.

1. The Immaculate Reception (I watched as a high school freshman in Buffalo, where the TV feed wasn't blacked out, and wow!).
2. Santonio Holmes's Super Bowl XLIII–winning touchdown reception.
3. James Harrison's 100-yard interception return for a touchdown in Super Bowl XLIII.
4. Antwaan Randle El's touchdown pass to Hines Ward in Super Bowl XL.
5. "Fast" Willie Parker's 75-yard touchdown run in Super Bowl XL.
6. Troy Polamalu's pick six to clinch the 2008 AFC Championship Game.
7. Eric Williams's pick-off of John Elway and subsequent return to the 2-yard line to set up the game-winning TD in the 1984 AFC Divisional playoffs.
8. Ben Roethlisberger to Mike Wallace for the game-winning touchdown at 0:00 to beat the Packers in 2009.
9. Antonio Brown's Immaculate Extension touchdown to beat the Ravens in 2016.
10. The Wizard of Boz, Chris Boswell's franchise-record 59-yard field goals in 2020 and 2022.

after a quick trot to the sideline and called a pass play, a quick button-hook. He said cryptically, "Break one tackle and it's six points." He knew the wide receiver, knew a blitz was coming, and knew the man in coverage. Sure enough, at the snap of the ball, Cliff dropped back and threw a quick strike into the slot. Lester Hayes jumped the route and stepped in front of the would-be receiver, intercepted the pass, broke a tackle by another Steeler, and took it into the end zone. As I was walking off the field, Larry Brown said simply, "Well, you gotta hand it to Cliff. He called it, even down to the 'break a tackle and it's six' part."

One of the all-time greatest Super Bowl plays I ever saw happened when the Steelers played Super Bowl XLIII in Tampa, winning spectacularly against the Arizona Cardinals and capping off their incredible 2008 season. I remember having a conversation with James Harrison a day later. He recounted his outstanding 100-yard interception return for a touchdown and explained why he dropped into coverage instead of rushing. Now this is a great example of what trusting your instincts is all about. He talked about being a step late on his pass rushes against Cardinals tackle Mike Gandy the entire first half. He just wasn't getting home in time.

I don't know what James knew with his samurai sixth sense in that Super Bowl. But in that moment, backed up against his own goal line with time running out in the half and facing Kurt Warner on the other side of the line of scrimmage with a slot receiver to his right and the threat of the quick slant, Deebo's sixth sense kicked in. His gut began talking to him. He knew instinctively that he wouldn't get to Warner before Warner could get the ball where he wanted it. Still, knowing that he was needed to create the threat of a rush so that Gandy didn't simply squeeze down on the inside gap, which would make life difficult for the blitzing Lawrence Timmons, Harrison faked a rush. In doing so, it caused Gandy to step out toward Harrison and honor the outside rush. Then James suddenly dropped into coverage. It was something that

Warner couldn't have anticipated, because in all likelihood, and with all respectful deference to Harrison's coverage abilities, his game was to get after the quarterback, not drop into coverage.

And James was right. Boy, was he ever. And what a return. Weaving, gaining blocks, swerving to make Cardinals miss, and finally crossing the goal line after the longest play in Super Bowl history, James cemented himself into everlasting fame—all because he listened to his gut instinct and had the courage to act on it. It's just what the great ones do. It's what Hall of Famers do. And James Harrison should be one of them someday.

I watched that magnificent and historic play from the opposite sideline. I saw James prone on the ground after scoring the touchdown. Steelers team doctor Jim Bradley immediately ran out to tend to him. James was on his back and Doc was on one knee looking over James while talking to him. After a moment or two, I saw James, from my sideline vantage point, reach up and push Dr. Bradley's face away. He'd obviously said something to him. After a while, James got to his feet and went immediately to the Steelers locker room. As you probably know, James's Herculean, marathon-like run had sucked up all the remaining time in the first half.

After halftime ended and the players came back to the bench area for the second half, I made my way over to find Dr. Bradley to satisfy my curiosity. I asked Dr. Bradley what Deebo had said to him and why he had shoved him away. Doc looked at me with a grin and said, "He told me to get outta his face. That I was sucking up all his oxygen!"

Samurai sixth sense with a touch of humor. A historic play, *and* a laugh.

CHAPTER 34

LIFE IN THE FAST LANE

I read and reread the note from team historian and *Steelers Digest* editor Bob Labriola, and my mind began to drift as my heart rate kicked up a beat or two. "Digest assignment: Playoff football. How is it different? How do players treat it versus regular-season football? Anecdotes. Let it fly."

Indeed.

Playoff memories from years back began to wash over me as I pondered the assignment. Playoff football. What is it that so completely occupies the players, the coaches, and the fans? What so thoroughly drives emotions and passions to the heights of frenzied anticipation when playoffs begin? There's only one answer: It's the quest for the big one. In the postseason, the philosophical, semi-apologetic "We'll get 'em next time" you hear in the wake of a loss gives way to the one-and-done Apollo Creed simplification: "There is no tomorrow! There is no tomorrow!"

Playoffs in Pittsburgh are special. They are perceived almost as a legacy passed on from father and mother to son or daughter. Steelers fans continually showed me snapshots of their Steelers rooms, complete with full Steelers memorabilia, and shared huge moments of their lives that surrounded a playoff game—weddings, funerals, and other mile-markers that occurred the day before or the day of a playoff game. The Steelers were a part of that family tradition and lore.

I remember Steelers fans and seemingly the entire city of Pittsburgh cresting to crescendo when the playoffs rolled around in January 1983 with the Chargers coming to town. Life suddenly kicked into another gear; the Steelers morphed the 'Burgh into the City of Champions, complete with banners, songs, and throngs. You immediately became aware that this was not business as usual.

When Chuck Noll addressed us at the beginning of the week, he uncharacteristically began by stating, "It's money time!" The vets acted differently, the coaches coached more fervently, and there was an unspoken acknowledgment among all of us that we were not in Kansas anymore. The Steelers had missed the playoffs my first two years, 1980 and 1981 (which had been especially bitter after the historic run of the '70s Steelers). The anticipation of "one for the thumb" had become the predominant catchphrase. It was everywhere, from the nightly news to the radio talk shows dominated by Myron Cope.

Preparation during the week took on heightened energy as the expectations grew and postseason play inched ever closer. It was my first playoff game, and I was a starter. I couldn't wait for kickoff. I'm telling you, wild horses couldn't have dragged me away from playing this game!

The week stretched on and on. I lived the game in my daily "theater of the mind" mental gymnastics, going over and over the scouting report. I reviewed game film of my opponent, Chargers DT Gary Johnson, daily. By night, I obsessively dreamed in living color of Johnson's big club move, with which he had sacked many a quarterback. I had to be strong with my left hand in pass pro.

And then it happened. On the last play of the last practice before that playoff game, I broke my thumb—my left thumb, of course. Fearing I'd be pulled from the starting lineup if I told anyone, I kept it to myself. I told the trainer I had just sprained it. Right before kickoff, I had it shot up with a painkiller. We had a saying back in the day: "The needle is your friend." And indeed it was.

But adrenaline is a player's *best* friend. And when we took the field that day at Three Rivers Stadium, I thought my head might explode from all the excitement pouring out of the stands and washing over us while we warmed up. It was truly one of the most incredible moments of my life. Standing among legends, I took in the moment. Jack Lambert. Terry Bradshaw. Franco Harris. Lynn Swann. Jack Ham. John Stallworth. Mike Webster. And Mel Blount. To be there with them all, it was just incredible.

So was the ending of the game: a devastating 31–28 loss. That's when I learned what the movie *The Wizard of Oz* would have looked like had the film been reversed color-wise. The city of Pittsburgh went from a teeming vibrancy of color and excitement and energy to dismal, wintry black and white overnight.

Playoffs on the road are tough duty. But there is something about going into an enemy city feeling like marauders trying to metaphorically pillage and burn. To destroy the opposition and steal a chance in the hunt for pro football's ultimate prize. There's a lot of fan energy waiting to be deployed against you. And the longer you're in town, the more you become aware of it.

So it was in 1983, when we rolled into California early and spent a week in late December/early January at Thousand Oaks to prepare for the Raiders. After a week of practice in the sunshine and balmy 70-degree weather, we took the field at the L. A. Coliseum before the biggest crowd I'd ever seen. More than 90,000 fans stood, roared, and poured energy onto the field like I'd never heard.

Playoffs on the road were simply a mirror of Pittsburgh in another NFL city (you know, minus all the Super Bowls). The home team just feels bulletproof. When the Chargers came to Pittsburgh in January 1983, we thought we were going to blow them away. The conversation in Pittsburgh had been to "bring on the California-dreamin' boys and we'll freeze them out in a January playoff game." We were cocky.

It was like that in Denver after we landed there for a 1984 playoff game. Tunch Ilkin, Pete Rostosky, and I went to a restaurant the night before the game. At some point it became apparent that we had been outed as players—players from *that* team, no less. Conversations around us began in whispered tones, and then grew louder, with touches of bravado, as the evening wore on. They were all about how the Broncos shouldn't even have to play the Steelers.

"Bring on the Dolphins," laughed a man at a nearby table as his wine glass was being refreshed. Apparently, the school of thought was that the Broncos should just proceed to the AFC Championship Game and play Miami and Dan Marino. Tomorrow's game against Pittsburgh was simply a waste of the Broncos' time. So it was with more than a touch of malevolent glee that I laughed as we ran off the field at Mile High Stadium, redolent in the aftermath of a Bronco-busting 24–17 victory. Despite the late hour of our arrival back in the 'Burgh, cold weather and all, we were greeted by nearly 10,000 fans at the airport.

Championship teams have championship-caliber players. But often, championship teams have Hall of Fame players capable of carrying their team. Such was the case in the 1984 AFC Championship Game in Miami against the Dolphins. As Tunch liked to say, "We didn't lose to a team. We lost to a Hall of Fame quarterback."

He was right. We scored early in the game following a long, grinding, and time-consuming drive. But Miami responded quickly. The Dolphins crossed midfield after two or three completions from Dan Marino. Legendary center Mike Webster got up off the bench, grabbed another Gatorade, walked the sideline, and yelled at the defense to just "slow down Marino long enough so we can get a drink!"

I remember thinking we were in real trouble when, on third-and-8, Jack Lambert blitzed untouched and creamed Marino. And Marino was still able to sidearm a throw on his way to the ground. It was caught by RB Tony Nathan for a first down. We lost 45–28 to the Marino Dolphins; Pittsburgh's own Marino beat us by throwing for 421 yards and 4 touchdowns.

Playoffs are always about coaching. And coaching is all about being real. Being real means accepting realities and limitations, not painting rosy solutions when there are none. That was the perspective we had when we found ourselves in the unfriendly confines of the Houston Astrodome in 1989. We were up against the Houston Oilers in the wild-card round of the playoffs.

After a Rod Woodson fumble recovery in overtime temporarily stopped a late surge by the Oilers, and we couldn't do anything offensively,

Chuck Noll faced a tough decision with the score knotted: try a 50-yard Gary Anderson field goal attempt, or punt the ball away and hope there was just enough gas left in a tired and fading defense. Noll, always the ultimate realist in assessing tough decisions, talked to defensive coordinator Rod Rust. And in what I can only describe as an unbelievably candid conversation, Rust provided the most honest coordinator's response to Chuck's pointed question I ever heard.

"Can we hold them if we punt?"

"We can't hold them again, Chuck," Rust said of his exhausted defense.

So Chuck sent out Gary Anderson, and the rest is history. We had pulled off a 26–23 upset win on the road. Just like that, the House of Pain, as the Oilers defense had begun calling the Astrodome that year, became the Oilers' personal house of pain. As the members of their field goal block unit lay strewn about on the Astrodome turf, Tunch, never one to let a smackdown opportunity pass him by, ran around yelling at the Oilers, "How's the pain now, baby?!"

With fan enthusiasm bubbling over following the sudden-death victory in Houston, Denver loomed on the horizon. It was a return to the Rocky Mountains and Mile High Stadium, where we'd prevailed five years earlier. Having experienced playoff success there may have produced a warm, fuzzy memory, but that's all it was. We knew we had work to do.

The flight into Denver was memorable, and something that couldn't be done now considering today's rigid airline regulations. But back in the day, you were allowed to walk into the cockpit and talk to the pilots. Sometimes you were invited to sit in the jump seat behind the pilot as the plane landed. As a double-digit-year veteran, it was my turn to sit in with the pilots when we landed in Denver. I'll never forget the Denver airport coming into view from miles away—and miles high in the air—with the panoramic splendor of the Rockies as a backdrop.

"We've got to stop Hoag!" The Broncos struggled in the 1989 playoffs with Merril Hoge (center), who later worked seamlessly with Tunch (left) and me as part of the Steelers broadcast team. Courtesy of the Pittsburgh Steelers

The game itself was also unforgettable. It was highlighted by Merril Hoge, who rushed for 120 yards. Merril was virtually unstoppable, and his rushing success caused Broncos safety Dennis Smith to melt down during the game and lose his cool. Smith began berating his own guys in the huddle during a timeout: "*We gotta stop Hoag! We gotta stop Hoag!*"

Tunch, overhearing Smith screaming at his teammates (and again, never one to let a smackdown opportunity pass him by), yelled back, "His name is *Hoge*, you idiot. It's Hoge!"

"Hoag, Hoge, who cares? We're making him look like Jim Brown!" Smith retorted.

Unfortunately for us, we lost the game 24–23 on a last-gasp dropped pass that could have turned the loss into a possible win. Having experienced the Rocky Mountain high as both a winner and a loser in the playoffs, it would turn out to be my last game with the Steelers.

Well, when you fall short of fan expectations, the fall can be precipitous. Unlike the playoff experience of 1984 when we were greeted by thousands upon our victorious return to the Pittsburgh airport, this time there was no crowd, no fans, and no cheering throng. Just the singular, lonely ticket-taker at the airport parking lot in the frigid early January morning.

Playoff games. Nothing like winning them.

CHAPTER 35

THAT FIRST HIT OF TV

I never had aspirations to get into broadcasting. Instead, I opened a boxing, martial arts, and athletic training center a couple years after I retired from professional football, and I was quietly going about my business. I loved it. The Martial Arts and Sports Complex was a great gym. Tunch had gone another route. A broadcast major at Indiana State University, from the moment he hung up his cleats, his path was clear.

Anybody who knows us—or perhaps you're getting to know us by reading this book, and you're surely picking it up—knows that Tunch and I were always close friends. Twin brothers from different mothers. Upon retirement, we didn't see each other quite as often as we had during our playing days, especially when the football season hit. In the off-season, when his time freed up and he wasn't covering games, we'd reload. But we had always been just a quick phone call or hop in the car away from each other.

Tunch would usually stop to train at MASC—he was pretty good with his dukes—and for a long time we would get in the ring and spar with each other. We were actually sparring partners, kind of like Apollo Creed and Rocky Balboa sparring in *Rocky III*. (Hey, nothing says "I love you, man!" more than punching it out in a boxing ring.)

And we'd go hard. Tunch, that jerk, actually broke my nose with a good right-hand shot once. I'm not kidding. We were in the ring, in my gym, as I was preparing to box against Eric "Butterbean" Esch in Gulfport, Mississippi. While leaning back against the ropes, I came forward with my hands a little lax and a little low. You know, just what I tell my fighters *not* to do. And like a good friend should when called upon to remind the other of his bad habits, Tunch cracked me one. But trust me, such favors went both ways over the years. If you looked closely, one of Tunch's ears was a little cauliflowered up. *Gotta keep the earmuffs up to defend those hooks to the head, Tunch!* That's just what brothers do for each other. Oh, it was fun. And whoever bled more had to pick up the lunch tab.

Tunch wasn't the only Ilkin to train at MASC. Over the years, his boys Tanner and Clay and his daughter Natalie all trained here. Tanner, Tunch's oldest son, could punch like a mule kicks. He used to make the heavy bags hop. So one day Tunch bopped into the gym. I was teaching and kibitzing when Tunch suggested that I should report from the sideline for the Steelers on game day.

Honestly, it really didn't even register at the moment. With Tunch in the booth along with Bill Hillgrove and Myron Cope, they didn't even have a sideline reporter for the Steelers Radio Network. Besides, what does a sideline guy even do?

I told Tunch nah, that I was fine working in my gym. I really wasn't interested. Besides, I didn't know much of anything about sports broadcasting, other than what I had been exposed to as a player. To me, it was just a guy with a microphone asking questions.

Then again, I had studied at Syracuse University, home of the well-known Newhouse School of Broadcasting and training ground of many a legendary broadcaster. So I'd probably be a natural, right? Marv Albert and Bob Costas are just a couple Newhouse graduates, but I had never even set foot inside the building. It looked nice from the outside. In fact, Tunch often described my Syracuse years by teasing, "Wolf's hardest subject was geography. He couldn't find his class." Well, I can't deny any of that. Full disclosure: I came up four credit hours short of graduation.

Tunch continued to put the reporting bug in my ear. "Just try it," he would say. And it sometimes sounded like fun. After all, we had roomed together on the road and in training camp for 10 years, so the travel with this job would bring back those good ol' days, with the bonus of not getting beat up. Well, eventually I grew comfortable with the idea, tried it, and the rest is history.

But it certainly didn't come off without some foibles along the way. I'll be the first one to admit, I do have that proverbial "face for radio." Mike Webster used to chide me that "Nobody will ever get you confused with Robert Redford." But every now and again a little TV work would come up. Once, well into radio broadcasting at this point with the old Fox Sports affiliate in Pittsburgh, a sparring partner of mine and long-time friend, Lonely Dog, came into the gym.

"Hey," Lonely Dog said, "I saw you on Fox Sports last night."

"Oh yeah. What'd you think?"

"You've put on what, 10 or 15 pounds, haven't you?"

It was a statement more than it was a question. I gave him that old line about how the camera adds like five pounds to the face.

"Well, how many cameras were they using?"

Frankly, I couldn't stop laughing at that one.

To me, radio is not only fun, it's easy. Unlike TV, there's no dress code, no makeup, and you certainly don't need pretty hair. Plus, as I think you know by now, the free food was a bonus. Of course, there's free food in TV too, but the entire scene takes some getting used to. Live audiences can make you tense, if you're not a longtime pro like, say, Bob Pompeani. He's as smooth as they come.

However, TV did ultimately become a part of my radio job. One of the first times occurred at training camp; I had to do a hit from the sideline during practice. Well, of course, there are a lot of people that go to training camp, and our cameraman wanted to put me in front of a live shot for effect. So I was on the spot. I had to remember my lines, and I grew nervous. I walked down to the practice field, tried to read the notes I'd scribbled on a napkin, and silently rehearsed my lines. As practice unfolded, I mumbled, squinted through the sweat pouring from my forehead, dried off, and started over.

My cameraman gave me a brief overview right before we went live, and as the crowd roared, I could feel my heart accelerate as a dose of nervousness shot through me. Now, I have played in front of tens of thousands of screaming fans in NFL stadiums across the country, with millions in the television audience looking on, but this was a live crowd,

After a shaky start in broadcasting, I became a Pittsburgh mainstay as a radio, TV, and print media icon. Courtesy of Brian Price/WDVE Radio

and I didn't have a helmet to hide under or a huddle to get lost in. There wasn't even a teammate to lean on! This was a solo shot.

I began to run through my lines again as the cameraman got his equipment set up. I must've looked like *Rain Man* babbling away as I rehearsed, made mistakes, re-rehearsed. My innards tightened and the vicious cycle of anxiety amplified. Fred Tice, my cameraman, was a veteran of many training camps. He'd covered NFL games and news on all sorts of programs; he was one of the top pros of our time. A great guy, Freddy didn't suffer fools and/or idiot ex-athletes. He was a true professional who demanded your best effort. And if you listened to Fred, you would do a great job. But you had to have thick skin if you worked with him.

On this day, both of us were suffering from the excessive heat and humidity in Latrobe. Sweat was pouring off his brow just like it was mine. (My excuse was rookie nerves; he had the legitimate difficulty of hoisting a 30-pound camera over his shoulder.) Finally, after watching me for a while, he shot me an are-you-ready-for-this? look.

Ummmm…I told him I needed a few more minutes.

At this point Fred began eyeballing me with his notorious stink-eye. I would come to know that look well while working with him through the years. I was trying his patience, and I could feel his clock ticking. Finally, he'd had enough and signaled me to take my place along the snow fence surrounding the field. The kindly folks along the fence called to me as I moved toward them. I tried to appear confident, pasting an I-got-this look on my face while stuffing notes into my pocket. I stood on my mark and faced the field with the fans at my back. Licking my lips nervously, holding the microphone just so, wiping the sweat from my brow, trying to appear knowledgeable and secure, I faced Fred and the bright camera light.

"Hi, everwybody! I'm Wraig Colfley up at Twaining Cramp and…"

How Elmer Fudd suddenly showed up, I had no idea.

Cut.

It took me three takes just to get my name right. Seriously.

Fred looked at me with that slightly amused expression and patiently asked me to do it again. More takes, more cuts. More takes, more cuts. Fred was losing his patience and the crowd was getting in on it. "Cut! Do it again!" they began to shout—followed, of course, by laughter. Much, much laughter.

A couple more attempts, a couple more screwups. At this point, Fred wasn't even trying to hide his disdain. "OK, amateur hour is up!" he barked.

But another go produced another flub. Sweat was now running down my back. Just when I thought Fred had reached his breaking point, I heard the faint sounds of encouragement. And, yep, I pulled it together and nailed it.

Wearing a wholly exasperated and slightly satisfied smile, Fred turned the camera off and gave me the thumbs-up. "Only 14 takes, Wolf!"

I let out an audible sigh as I sank back and leaned on the fence. The tension suddenly left me and I felt hands tap my shoulders. I turned to see a group of women who had been watching me. I figured they were the ones who had offered up the "encouraging" words as I fumbled along.

As the group of 15 or so ladies circled to the sides, one looked at me very sincerely, patted me on the back, and said, "We were praying for you, dear. We didn't think you were going to be able to do it."

Truthfully, neither did I.

CHAPTER 36

NO SLITHERING AWAY

I'm really not a pet person. I did have a goldfish once, but he went belly-up. Oh, I also had a Japanese fighting fish in college. And I'm pretty sure a diet that at times consisted of Double Stuf Oreos gave him bad cholesterol. He turned into a floater too.

Now, my wife and kids, they're different. My wife, Faith, grew up on a farm and is a natural-born dog lover. And I'll tell you, I fell in love all over again when I saw her jump up on my sister's horse, riding bareback no less, wearing cutoff jeans and riding like she was born to do it. That'll grab a man's heart, and it surely did mine. I think, if given her druthers, she would have a lot more critters. Her mom tells a story of Faith as a little girl. Apparently she had to be snatched up from the zoo because she wanted to "pet the little kitty," which was actually a big ol' tiger. Yep, that's my girl Faith!

And my sister Linrae, well, she's always loved animals. She has a cattle farm and raises grass-fed cows, and has horses, dogs, and more. Faith introduced our daughter Megan to horses when she was just a little one. And for Megan, it was love at first sight.

But me? Nope. I wasn't born with that animal-lover gene. It skipped me entirely. We have dogs at home, Jake and Toto. And don't get me wrong, I love those idiots. But I don't act like they're one of my six kids, or grandkids for that matter.

Most critters don't bother me much, but I tend to keep my distance. I've had a horse step on my foot and had a giraffe spit at me. I once sat on a bull in a rodeo chute in Fort Worth—that was something. But there's one animal that I truly don't like. And I mean really. I *really* don't like snakes. Especially big snakes, like those you see in *National Geographic*, or read about under screaming headlines like: "Python Killed After Eating Half of Village."

Strangely enough, I used to hunt, capture, and keep garden-variety snakes as a kid growing up in Orchard Park. But those were the skinny little guys that are so small a big fly could choke them out. By the time I was an adult, I couldn't stand them.

Unless, of course, they were on boots, belts, and cowboy hats. Enter my urban cowboy phase. You see, coming to the Steelers and being introduced to real cowboys like Jon Kolb and Mel Blount, and guys like Terry Bradshaw and Tom Beasley who grew up on farms and around horses—well, they were a big influence. And so were their clothes.

On my first trip to Dallas, to play the Cowboys in a preseason game, I heard scuttlebutt that some of the guys were heading to a cowboy boot wholesaler. Someone had an in and we could get great deals on expensive boots. We landed the day before the game, had our special teams meeting at the hotel, and bused off to practice to "work the trip out of us," as Chuck used to say. We didn't have team meals after practices back then, so we could either order room service or head out to a restaurant. The only kicker would be bed check, when coaches knocked on your door to make sure you weren't burning the midnight oil.

Now, I didn't go to the boot wholesaler on this particular night. I was a rookie, and it was understood to be a veterans-only trip. But the next day a bunch of guys had brand-new snakeskin, ostrich skin, elephant skin, or alligator boots. A few had some really neat snakeskin patterns, too—python, anaconda, rattlesnake. I loved them, and when I could afford to, I bought some for myself. But that was as close to snakes as I ever wanted to get.

Some years later, during an off-season, the Steelers sent me to a park in West Virginia for a meet-and-greet. There, the park rangers hosted a wildlife petting zoo as part of the celebration. Knowing that my nine-year-old Megan would love it, I took her with me and we made it a fun daddy-daughter date. It was a beautiful summer afternoon drive. The place was crowded with Steelers fans, and of course West Virginia University fans as well. My brothers Ronny and Dale played at WVU, so

I had much in common with all the good folks who came out to see "the critters." We spent some time talking ball.

All was going well throughout the afternoon, until we came to the picnic area. There were goats, chickens, some horses—you know, the usual stuff you'd see at petting zoos. Sheep and cows, that kind of thing. But there was also an area that held the exotic, or not-so-usual critter. You know—a gator, a fox, or maybe a…python?

Oh boy. I knew there was going to be trouble the moment I saw that big ol' slithery thing. I spotted a sign that said something about getting your picture taken with it. *Nope. That ain't happening. Not with the kid here.*

I turned to her and said, "So, Megan, where are the ducks?"

But I knew who would want to take a picture with a python wrapped around her shoulders. *Megan.* "Dad! Look," she practically screamed as I tried to unsuccessfully guide her to another part of the petting zoo.

"Honey, how about a picture with a cute potbellied pig or soft, cuddly, little lamb?"

Nope. It had to be this nasty 12-foot, satanic-looking belly slider who looked big enough to eat the pig, the lamb, and singlehandedly make a complete smorgasbord buffet of half the petting zoo.

Mind you, this occurred over 30 years ago, but it still gives me the creeps today. And I mean to tell you this python was *BIG.* He had eyes that bored into you with a look that said, *So, you like snakeskin boots and belts, do ya?*

The snake was in a big box with high sides. Despite my reluctance, Megan dragged me over to the side of it. The handler smiled warmly and engaged Megan in conversation. I stood stupidly by, mesmerized by the unfolding coils of snake before me. I listened to him explain to Megan how many rats a week it devoured. I nodded stiffly when he pointed out certain characteristics, such as how they smelled through their tongue. I attempted a half-hearted joke about a python-skin belt, that I, uh, had… or…ummm….

A band of brothers: (left to right) Ronnie, Dale, and me.

The snake dude looked at me like I had two heads. The whole snakeskin belt small talk wasn't going over well with the snake handler or the snake, who looked like he was ready for a rat or three. Meanwhile, Megan, rapt with joy, was totally oblivious to my struggles. But I was just trying not to scream in sheer panic. C'mon, I watch National Geographic. I've seen them eat mice and put chokeholds on other animals. All I could do was stare at that monstrous python. My skin was crawling.

"Dad, let's get a picture with us holding the python!" said Megan gleefully. She was completely absorbed in the thought of how her friends would think it was so cool for her to have that snake sitting on her skinny little shoulders. I don't think Megan had any idea how heavy this monster was.

"C'mon, Meg, that's ridiculous. I'm sure that's not allowed. We can just stand by the side here and somebody can get a shot."

The wrangler looked at Megan, then me, and with a little twist of sarcasm in his voice and a knowing tilt of his head, said, "No problem, Megan."

I knew it. Revenge of the python.

In her excitement, Megan didn't even notice she was getting those "dad eyes," which usually pulled her in like a *Star Wars* tractor beam. Nope, she was full steam ahead, baby.

"All right, all right!" Megan was hopping around and excitedly yelling to anyone who would listen that she was going to get her picture taken with a python and her dad. I began making up silly and increasingly more stupid reasons not to do it. Mr. Snakeman, though, wasn't helping. His amused expression challenged every one of my lame excuses. Megan began to pick up the dynamic.

"Dad, are you afraid?" she asked. There. With the little voice that I so dearly loved and adored, Megan had nailed it. A slight look of disbelief, maybe even astonishment, began creeping over her little face. She was my firstborn, my fair-haired, beloved, and outrageously cute little girl. And there she was, looking at me with those big blue eyes and sensing something that I couldn't possibly admit to, at least not in front of her: that yes, Daddy was afraid.

I laughed nervously and waved off her slightly sorrowful question with an air of phony courage. "Of course not, baby girl!" I realized I was muttering to myself about how ridiculous it was that Dad was afraid of a snake. I made sure not to make eye contact with Mr. Snakeman either. I was just hoping he wouldn't out me at this point.

To think that I, a professional football player, a man who had gone eyeball-to-eyeball with the likes of Lawrence Taylor, Reggie White, and Howie Long, was afraid of a snake. *I mean seriously, Megan. I'm your dad; I'm not afraid of anything!*

So I tried to rally. Maybe I could get a shot of courage and paste a smile on my face. After all, Megan was looking at me with eyes that a daddy would never want to disappoint. Against my far better judgment, I agreed to do it.

Mr. Snakeman was almost gleeful as he picked up that diabolical, coiling nightmare from another world and gestured for me to turn around. In what may have been the slowest turnaround in the history of turning around, I obliged him. And to this day I can still feel the slithery skin of that python as its scales made contact with the back of my neck. If I could have jumped out of my skin, I would have set a record for skin jumping.

In a final coup de grâce, the snake handler put the head of the snake in my right hand and made me hold that thing right where the ears would have been if it'd had ears on its head. And it was a big head, I tell you.

Megan, looking for all the world like she was in nirvana, was so excited she could barely contain herself. She gleefully waited as Mr. Snakeman draped the back end of the snake over her little shoulders.

I probably bore 70 to 75 percent of the snake's considerable weight and length on my shoulders. With a dire sense of impending doom, I watched as the snake's tongue darted in and out hypnotically.

Great. Googly. Moogly. It was at that moment, hoping beyond hope that I was anywhere but there, the snake moved. *Rippled* might be a better word for it. Seriously. This thing rippled! And the powerful, wavelike muscular contractions of its body made me shudder. And almost bolt.

I kid you not. If Megan hadn't been there, and wasn't so joyously looking at me, I would've been so long gone. It took every ounce of my shredded manhood and self-esteem to keep from screaming out in sheer panic. And at that exact moment, Mr. Snakeman snapped that picture. I wasn't even aware it'd happened. I don't remember anyone saying "look over here, say cheese, smile"—nothing.

Thankfully, that photo has been lost to the decades. But I have a feeling that somewhere, down in the garage, in some long-lost photo album, that picture is there. Me, holding a giant python, and a bubbly little blonde-haired girl wearing a smile normally reserved for a shopping mall Santa.

And her father? Well, if you looked up *terror* in the dictionary, you'd see that face. And no words would be necessary.

Megan and me. Courtesy of Dean Elliott

AFTERWORD

BY KYLE WOLFLEY

Back when I was teaching at West Point and wanted to break the ice on the first day of class, I would ask my students to say something interesting about themselves. To get us started, I offered to go first, and explained that my dad played in the NFL as a lineman for over a decade. Their reaction? "Sir, your dad played professional football? What happened to *you*?" Well, I told them, although I was not blessed with his physical stature, I sure did inherent his dancing skills. (Somehow my students didn't think it was as funny as I did.) Perhaps I'll let my wife, Danessa, be the judge of that.

As a matter of fact, it was my dad who introduced me to Danessa, about 14 years ago. I flew home for Christmas from my first duty station in Germany, and my dad picked me up from the airport. During our ride home, he casually noted, "Hey, Kyle, there's this really nice girl, with a wonderful family, that we met at church in Harrisville. I think the two of you should meet."

My dad wore his heart on his sleeve, so I wasn't shocked that he was attempting to meddle in my romantic life. But at the same time, I felt the need to push back: "Dad, are you really trying to play matchmaker for me?" He responded, "I'm just looking out for my eldest son, who I love dearly."

As I held my dad's hand while he lay in his hospital bed the week before he passed, I reminded him of this story. He looked at Danessa and said, "That was one of the best things I ever did." However, it may turn out that the original idea to introduce me and my bride-to-be originated from my stepmom, Faith. But as my dad would say, "Never let facts get in the way of a good story!"

Yet it is a fact that my father's contributions to this world—and the number of people he touched—are so vast that if we wrote them down, we would fill up a stadium. To name just a few of his accomplishments: He was selected to the Syracuse All-Century Team and Greater Buffalo Sports Hall of Fame; was a top competitor at the World's Strongest Man competition; and remained a stalwart of the Pittsburgh Steelers offensive line for 10 years. On the air as a broadcaster, his enthusiasm and extensive vocabulary captured the hearts of Steelers Nation around the world. He would often exclaim "Gadzooks!" at big plays and encouraged players get their "mojination" going.

But for my dad, these achievements were secondary to his most important mission. To him, what mattered most were the opportunities to mentor and serve others: men's Bible study at churches around Pittsburgh, outreach programs like Man Up, and especially the work of the Light of Life Rescue Mission. There, he served Thanksgiving dinner, supported those in most need, and led the annual walk with my "uncle" Tunch Ilkin. My dad was the best example of a servant leader that I ever encountered, and he loved sharing God's message with all.

From a young age, my dad instructed me to be strong and courageous, instilling in me Joshua 1:9 to firm up my confidence. I was enthralled by his stories of grit on the field, where he battled every Sunday with the toughest men in God's creation. Yet the strength that he taught was paired with a sense of duty to love without end. He exemplified an unmatched compassion toward others.

When I was in elementary school, it was common for my dad to (gently) bump heads with me as a symbol of our bond together before parting ways. One day when he picked me up from kindergarten, a teacher approached him and asked, "Mr. Wolfley, is it true that you headbutt your son before school?" I can still imagine my dad's face turning bright red. At the Light of Life mission, I witnessed him in action: not headbutting (maybe thankfully) but hugging, praying, and sometimes crying. No matter what, he sought to comfort and witness Christ's love to those in need.

That was my dad, the gentle giant who was larger than life, and his heart was too big for this world. He treated every person he encountered as if they were the most important he'd ever met. Those he crossed paths with would call him friend, mentor, and brother. He served as a father figure for so many that I feel blessed to count dozens of other men as my brothers. He smiled, he hugged, he lit up the room, and he shared the Gospel. His passion for the Lord was evident to everyone he encountered. He once confided in me that Christ's salvation was like "the cure for cancer," something so life-saving that it could not be kept a secret.

In what felt like an instant, I lost my dad, best friend, and hero. We who were blessed to know him now have a Wolf-sized hole in our hearts. But I imagine him in heaven with his brothers—Uncle Tunch and Uncle Dale—locked in arms, encouraging me to share with you that he is with Jesus, our Lord and Savior, and is laughing that big laugh that we all love and miss. Only Christ can fill a hole this big in our hearts.

Dad, thank you for the love that you gave unconditionally. Thank you for your example as a leader, husband, and father. I will miss you dearly, and I will never be the same without you. But I know you would tell us we have more work to do: to carry out the work of Christ and to love without ceasing.

—Kyle Wolfley

ACKNOWLEDGMENTS

BY FAITH WOLFLEY

Knowing my Bear, he would first and foremost want to thank his Lord and Savior, Jesus Christ, for all the amazing blessings and opportunities He provided for him. Craig adored and was so proud of all our children—Megan, Kyle, Craig Jr. (CJ), Maximos, Esther, and Hannah—for being the greatest gifts from God and the inspiration for so many of these stories.

Oh, how he loved his family! Craig's mom, Hoopy—or as he often called her, "a human rose"—was his rock, guiding light, and biggest cheerleader throughout his entire life. His siblings, whom he lovingly

Craig will be missed by all. He gets a hug here from next-generation Steeler Brett Keisel (right) at the Mel Blount Roast. Courtesy of the Pittsburgh Steelers

called Linirae (Linrae), Ponyboy (Ron), Joycee-may (Joy), and Sodapop (Dale), were as vital a part of his life as he was to theirs. They also have been an inspiration for so many of these stories.

And the game he loved so much: football. And via that family, that team, that Steelers Nation, football loved him back just as much. Of the teammates who had bonds thicker than blood and became family, that list is too long to write. But if he did, his brother in Christ, his best friend and teammate Tunch Ilkin would be at the top of it.

Oh, how he loved to tell these stories! This book has been several decades in the making, and without Jim Wexell's dedication, encouragement, and hard work, it would have never made it to completion. Craig was so thankful for how Jim continually encouraged him to write and published his articles in his online publication, *SteelCityInsider*. Craig respected Jim as a mentor and fellow writer, but more importantly as a great friend.

As so many of you know, Craig loved people. He loved to encourage, entertain, build up, and motivate anyone who crossed his path in life. He never thought of a person as just a fan but as a friend. His friends gave him the ability to do what he loved to do: tell stories from inside the locker room, down on the sideline, inside the huddle, and right there on the line of scrimmage. And as the laughter erupted, he loved to say, "Never let facts stand in the way of a good story!"

—Faith Wolfley

73